The Last Days According to Jesus' Family

The Last Days According to Jesus' Family

The Story We Left Behind

BY

M. L. Banzhaf

FOREWORD BY

Franklin Pyles

RESOURCE *Publications* • Eugene, Oregon

THE LAST DAYS ACCORDING TO JESUS' FAMILY
The Story We Left Behind

Resource Publications
An Imprint of Wipf and Stock Publishers
199 W. 8th Ave., Suite 3
Eugene, OR 97401

www.wipfandstock.com

PAPERBACK ISBN: 979-8-3852-7429-1
HARDCOVER ISBN: 979-8-3852-7430-7
EBOOK ISBN: 979-8-3852-7431-4

VERSION NUMBER 04/02/26

All Bavli citations are to *The Talmud: The Steinsaltz Edition* (New York: Random House, 1989–1999) unless otherwise noted. Rabbinic citations follow standard abbreviations: b. = Babylonian Talmud; m. = Mishnah; t. = Tosefta. Citations are given by tractate and folio (e.g., b. Berakhot 28b–29a) or by tractate and section (e.g., m. Yoma 8:6; t. Berakhot 3:25). Citations to the *Shulchan Arukh* are by section and paragraph (e.g., *Yoreh De'ah* 321:1). When a passage is consulted online (e.g., Sefaria), the platform and access date are noted in the relevant endnote.

Qur'an citations and English translation. Unless otherwise noted, Qur'anic quotations and translations are taken from Saint Murad, Quran ~ Saint Murad Translation (English digital edition, PDF/Kindle) 2024. Qur'anic references follow the standard sūrah:āyah format (e.g., Q 3:50; 5:46–48). When used, tafsīr refers to the classical and later Qur'anic commentary/exegesis tradition that interprets the text and supplies narrative, lexical, and theological explanation.

"Banzhaf courageously challenges readers to reconsider the stories that have shaped our imagination. Mary and her family, and the early Jewish followers of Jesus, are not tribal weapons meant to justify hostility. They are invitations to rediscover God's covenantal purposes—purposes rooted in mercy, faithfulness, and the restoration of relationship. . . . For those of us who live in the land where these biblical stories took place, the questions raised in this book are not abstract theological debates. They shape how Christians understand their neighbors, how they pray for peace, and how they embody the gospel in a fractured world. The church does not serve the kingdom of God by amplifying division. Rather, we serve Christ when we become witnesses to his reconciling love. If this book helps the church rediscover that calling—even in small ways—it will have served the gospel well. May these pages encourage readers to seek truth, pursue mercy, and remember that the story of God has always been, and will always be, a story of family gathered by grace."

—**Jack Sara**, President, Bethlehem Bible College

"It was not only a great pleasure but also a deep learning experience to host Martin Banzhaf on The Meaning Code YouTube channel back in 2022. Major kudos that he has written a book that puts these ideas together in a compelling format, and so beautifully written as to be almost poetic."

—**Karen Wong**, Host, The Meaning Code

"In this warm and heartfelt book, Marty has woven personal memoir, historical research and theological reflection into a narrative that asks the reader to put aside dogmatics and enter instead into the story of God for the world. Using the *Torat Edom*—a concept that many in the Evangelical world will do well to comprehend—Marty has provided a framework for understanding the last days that focuses on lived experience rather than the abstract countdown of eschatological events. Indeed, we are reminded that the last days are better read not as the triumph of Christians over other religions, particularly those of Judaism and Islam, but the story of the covenant God who is fulfilling his covenant promises. In following the example of Jesus' own family—through expressing mercy (Mary), faithfulness (James), and perseverance (Jude), we better reflect the heart of God for all of humanity. With personal prose and accounts of his own upbringing as a refugee and later missionary work providing a real-world grounding, Marty exhorts us to live as citizens of the coming kingdom in the present—even as we await its ultimate unveiling."

—**Peter Laughlin**, Chair, International Commission of Theological Education, Alliance World Fellowship

"M. L. Banzhaf's study invites readers to examine the traditions surrounding early Christianity with careful attention to their historical and theological context. As a student of Rabbi Eliyahu Benamozegh, whose *Israel and Humanity* envisioned a constructive relationship between Judaism and Christianity, I welcome works that pursue serious and respectful engagement and help renew our shared scriptural heritage."

—**Ben Abrahamson**, Director, Al-Sadiqin Institute

"Marty opens our eyes to see past centuries of Western church, back to *ekklesia* rooted in family, around tables, in community. Rich insight into Jesus' own family and Jewish community, and capable detangling of years of empire, church, and forced eschatology, lead us see—and be—the faithful people of God in fellowship and on mission in these last days."

—**Tim Crouch**, Vice President for Alliance Missions, The Christian and Missionary Alliance

"In *The Last Days According to Jesus' Family*, M. L. Banzhaf invites readers to reconsider the end not as a timeline to decode, but as a covenantal story to inhabit. With careful attention to Scripture, history, and lived experience, he offers a vision shaped less by fear and more by humility, healing, and hope. This is a thoughtful and needed contribution for those seeking a deeper, more faithful reading of the biblical narrative of the last days."

—**Hunter Barnes**, Host, Daily Radio Bible Podcast

"Banzhaf weaves his own spiritual journey throughout this book with both theological rigor and pastoral sensitivity, addressing divisive issues such as Christian nationalism, dispensationalism, and replacement theology, not to inflame controversy, but to heal theological fractures. The result is not so much mind blowing as mind stretching—a work that invites pastors and scholars alike to think beyond our traditional and popular frameworks and calls the church back to A. B. Simpson's 'center of gravity: a Christ-shaped theology ordered toward mission.' The appendices and Franklin Pyle's foreword are essential reading as capstones for the book."

—**Paul L. King**, Ordained Pastor, The Christian and Missionary Alliance

For Gloria:

"Your young man saw visions,
and your old man dreams dreams."

(Joel 2:28; Acts 2:17)

Contents

Foreword

BY Franklin Pyles

THE EARLY TWENTIETH-CENTURY PROTESTANT Church in America was convulsed with controversies over the Social Gospel, the founding of new seminaries, and debates over the relationship of the Bible and science. These matters deserve their place of privilege in any account of that era. But just over the ecclesial horizon another development was rising—one that would shape not only American Protestantism but Protestant and Roman Catholic churches worldwide: the modern resurgence of interest in prophecy, and with it a renewed focus on the Jewish people and their longing for a homeland.

After World War I, the Middle East was carved up, and Britain assumed control of Palestine—an event that made prophecy teachers hopeful. Then one of the most evil efforts since Haman arose like a beast in Germany, intent on obliterating Jews from the earth. After its material—but not spiritual—defeat, Allied public opinion shifted toward granting the Jewish people a homeland: what is now the State of Israel. Yet, as I write, antisemitism is again raising its ugly head—and some Christians are complicit.

That complicity does not always arise from "replacement theology," the belief that God's use of Israel to bring blessing to the nations has ended and that the church has replaced Israel in God's economy. Antisemitism is not a necessary outcome of replacement theology, but it can provide a ready plank in a platform when one seems to be needed by those who perpetually hate the Jewish people.

By the 1970s, prophecy became an industry in the United States. Marty Banzhaf speaks of how mass media empowered it to form tribalism and, ultimately, fear of the other. While antisemitism has quietly reemerged, the heirs of the early prophecy conferences have also promoted a message that collapses Jewish identity into modern statehood: that the State of Israel and the Jewish people are the same, and that to oppose the actions of the State of Israel is to oppose the Jewish people. Social media amplifies this with images of Israel as a lion and with Bible verses about blessing—often while ignoring the destruction and outright persecution of the Palestinian people. The result is a deep animosity toward Arab people that is both racial and religious.

Racial, because Palestinians are Arabs and the West has long had a fraught relationship with Arab peoples. Religious, because many Arabs identify as descendants of Ishmael, and the Abraham-and-Ishmael story has often been misread as a perpetual religious warrant for animosity. What has been true through the ages is true here again: once a "religious reason" is claimed for actions, almost anything becomes permissible—especially if violence is framed as aiding the fulfillment of prophecy.

It is as if a hockey game were growing increasingly violent and fans began to don their own skates, jumping onto the ice to join in the battle, referee whistles notwithstanding. Is there any way to stop this mayhem and still have hockey—and its rules—at the end? Is there any way to take the prophetic writings seriously, as Scripture demands, while avoiding the tribalism and fear that hold such a tenacious grip on American evangelicalism? Can mercy be found again?

For Marty, the Israel/Palestinian divide is a wound within the covenantal family of God. That wound becomes the entry point for considering other fractures as well: between evangelicals and Roman Catholics, Muslims, and Jews—wounds—and the implications of these fractures for the gospel. It is not that these wounds must be healed before there can be a faithful announcement of the good news. That would be an idealistic assessment—one which A. B. Simpson the founder of The Christian & Missionary Alliance would likely have identified as an outgrowth of postmillennialism. Rather, the pursuit of healing is itself part of the church's vocation in announcing the gospel.

It might be tempting to assume Marty will simply urge appreciation, dialogue, and getting along—another well-wisher. But he calls for something more demanding: a radical rethinking of the foundational stories—Mary, Abraham and Ishmael, Jacob and Esau, James, Jude, and Paul—and then an explication of those stories and their implications for the announcement of the gospel.

The spread of the good news—of Jesus who has come, has died, has risen, and who will come again—is at the heart of all theology. That the gospel, the announcement of the Father's love (John 3:16), must be proclaimed to every person on earth—and that this proclamation belongs to the work of the last days—was foundational to the development of a robust theology of mission. A. B. Simpson took an early step in that direction by expounding Matthew 24:14: the end will come when this gospel of the kingdom has been preached to all the world.

Marty maintains that seeing the theological importance of Jesus' family helps us understand that the end-time work of the church is not a break with God's historic covenantal work, but the widening of it to all peoples. In effect, he is laying another plank in the theology of mission: why missionary work is done, and how it is to be done.

Since Simpson, missiology has developed considerably, especially in articulating evangelism and mission as participation in the mission of God: God saw our distress, heard our cry, and came in love in the person of Jesus Christ to save us. This depth should help us understand mission as a last-days project precisely because it is not different from the covenant God made with Israel, but the fulfillment of promises embedded in the prophetic writings: that the nations would be gathered into the covenant, that there would be one people of God.

The end is the inclusion of the peoples of the earth into a covenant home where both the redeemed community and the redeemed individual are held together—where personal sins are washed away by the blood of the cross, and a people is formed in righteousness. Both are necessary goals of mission.

Mary and her song forge this link between covenant and the work of the last days, for she celebrates the mercy of God and announces what is about to be revealed in its fullness through the birth of her child—mercy in all its fullness.

The church's efforts to communicate the gospel—to be true ambassadors rather than arriving as conquerors—have had mixed results throughout history. Yet the theology and practice of mission did grow. Western missionaries increasingly recognized that many cultures are not individualistic like the modern West; in many places communities decide together. This helped give rise to "people movements," where thousands moved into faith. Yet the old divides—between Islam and Christianity, and between Judaism and Christianity—remain.

Much more needs to be done. Here, in this study, a meaningful step is taken: mission is rooted again in the ancient stories and in the ancient action of God to save.

Marty urges us not to avoid the wound between evangelicals and others, but to step into it—just as Jesus stepped into the ancient wound between Samaritans and Jews when he arrived at Jacob's well, waiting for a certain woman. She expressed her expectation in the language of prophecy: "We know that Messiah will come." Jesus did not belittle her, create fear, or reinforce the tribal walls that separated Jews from Samaritans. He showed mercy and clarified fulfillment: "The time is coming and now is." The end time is here. The time for salvation is here. And she, in turn, became an announcer—an evangelist.

Prophecy is not given to make us afraid of the antichrist, as real as he will be, but to fill us with hope: that the Lord's grace will tear down ancient barriers and that the light of the gospel will illumine every dark corner of every people, so that long-festering wounds can be healed.

In a moment when power, hatred, and hierarchy are being proclaimed by a new paganism as the solution to the world's problems, the church must again study the meaning of the last days and realize they are not an escape plan but a covenantal summons: to walk in the Name, refuse counterfeit kingdoms, bring healing to ancient wounds, live now as citizens of the City that is coming, and announce the coming of Jesus.

Franklin Pyles has pastored a number of churches, taught theology, and served as president of the Christian and Missionary Alliance in Canada.

Acknowledgments

Along with Gloria, I am grateful to the Lord for our whole family—across Ohio, Peru, Brazil, Canada, and Germany. They mean everything to us. We want to honor my wonderful mother, Christel, a "war hero" who saved her little brother and sister from a burning ship in Danzig Harbor while fleeing the former East Prussia in 1944, as we offer this book in memory of our little brother, Herb.

To all the former members of Erin Avenue Baptist Church on Cleveland's near west side in the late 1960s—later Redeemer Baptist Church in Parma, Ohio. And the Swampers in Sweet Home North Olmsted Smashing Pumpkins and burning Christmas Trees around 1979.

We also thank our cousins Laurie Melchien Reeves for comments on the manuscript (and her boys), and Pastor Tammy Melchien—who inspired me after her recent book, *Choose the Opposite* (NavPress). We are deeply grateful, for their parents, who have faithfully encouraged and prayed for Gary and Christel and their boys: Tante Barb, the youth pastor at Erin Avenue Church, and my Onkel Horst, who served in church leadership at Redeemer and sang in the choir—respective examples of victory in Jesus and the imitation of Him.

We are grateful for the many places where we have served.

First, for our Operation Mobilization (OM) ship family on the MV *Doulos* (1983–87), the MV *Hannah* (Barnabas & Young Ran Park) , and the MV *Logos II* (1991–95)—and especially for old shipmates who read the manuscript, including Susana Molina Gretschmann, Gert Jan Weekhout, Markus Vanilau, Roberta Johansson, Kevin Boehmer, and Carlos Torres, with loving memory of Liliana Torres (1956–2022) and Neisa Pamfil (1956–2016). And my first OM teammates in 1984 in Judenburg,

Austria. God really does make all things beautiful in His time . . . as the mountains still call me.

Second, for Star of Hope and others in Sweden—Bjorg and the Eriksson family; the late mother to many Brazilian orphans, Ulla Brit Sundstrom; Maine Viklund Olafsson; Barbro Jonsson Wallhäger and Amos Kevin Annan; Petra College of Children Ministry South Africa, Ana and Oskar Pon Zapata; and Ulriksberg Kyrkan in Växjö, Sweden—and all the projects around the world where they continue to aid children.

Third, for Iglesia Alianza Cristiana y Misionera in Peru, who first sent us and supported our work in Italy; and for all the members we left behind in Rome—Fondazione Belem (Tione di Trento), the Filipino Alliance Church of Bologna, Milan Bible Church, and our friends and co-workers in Milan and Bergamo, including Andrea, Blade, Davide and Francesca, and Giordano. Cross Point Alliance Church in Minnesota for partnership in the work in Italy. Plus our Alliance Mission Leaders Tim Crouch, Al Stombaugh, Bao Her and our European Leaders Ed and Julie Mangham plus the fields of Spain and Portugal, Alliance Diaspora Ministries; CAMA Zending Holland and the leaders of the Alliance World Fellowship.

I'm also thankful for the places where I studied—not merely as institutions, but as formative communities: Prairie Bible Institute (1987–89), Reformed Theological Seminary (1995–97), Norwich University (2007–09), and Warner University; and in Rome, the Angelicum and the Salesianum—where Ada and Federica as fellow students and Bishop Cornelius Onyigbuo and many other clergy provided comradery in a challenging academic environment.

Over the last decade, I'm thankful for the surprising gifts of "online halls"—especially the Alliance theology conversations where I first met Franklin Pyles and Paul King—and for all of us who still have a lot to learn about the legacy of A. B. Simpson. and, in more recent years, Peter Laughlin and the Alliance Theological Symposium. And to our Alliance friends in Brazil, and to the churches and seminary in Puerto Rico where parts of this work were first shared.

I'm grateful as well for friendships that became classrooms: Leonardo De Chirico, and the Rome Leaders and Scholars Network; the memory of the Dominican scholar Padre Walter Senner (1948–2020); and finally my Jewish teachers—Hakan Yossi, those in Bei Abedan, Rabbi Ben Abrahamson, and in memory of Yeshayahu (Ha Kohen) Hollander (yahrzeit: Tishrei 5786 — September 24, 2025).

We are grateful for our long-time partners in Orlando: our "big sister," Judy, and Bart Johnson; and for the memory of Mama Jewel and Q.R.; for David and Martha Castor; Joe and Rita Creech; David and Maggie Moore; Robin Cole; Stan Pietkiewicz; and all the members and pastors at Orangewood Presbyterian Church, where I served as an elder. I'm grateful for our missions prayer group in the 90s and SALT—in memory of Nancy Moore—and, last but not least, for the inspiration we received from Rev. Dr. H. Charles Green ("Chuck," 1946–2017) and Linda, the church's visionary founder.

We also want to acknowledge our supporters through the years—from Florida to Ohio—including Tim and Rene Burtrum and Tony; Brian and Trudy Fluck; Steven and Sharon Bozarth; Doug and Gay Fleming; Ed and Mary Rivera; Jeff and Dawna Riley; Heath and Elizabeth; Kevin Rambo; Chris and Camille Bassil; Nilza Guzman; Amadeo "Kiko" and Rosana Torres; Jaime and Suzy Chavez; Phil and Nita Stalnaker; Irene and Frank Williamson; Becky Carpenter in memory of Alan; Rick Heaton; Sophi Kim; Jon and Dana Houser; Don Aldrich (who also read the manuscript); Scot and Nancy Post; Mark and the memory of Gail Howland Hoover; Harry and Linda Bound; Steve and Monika Parker; Tom and Ginny Cressman; Sandy Schurdell; Tom and Zay Ziegler; Zoe Rodriguez; Axel and Rutinha Lanausse; Ralph and Marylyn Kuivinen; and in memory of Bruno and Eva Kiepke, Karl and Ingrid Fladda, Arnold and Rita Lowe, Willy and Mary Fast, Adolf and Erna Sonntag, Bert and Edith Wildner, Marlene Willis, Gladys and Phylis—and for many global prayer warriors too numerous to count.

We are grateful, too, for the more recent churches that support us now in the Alliance Southeast District (Florida), and that Hermana Ruth Volstad Davidson—Gloria's teacher many years ago in Ecuador—is nearby. And now, through Bob and Karen Formica and John and Lisa Sappia, we are connected to Village Church at Shell Point, DeLand Alliance Community (Joyce Houck and Raymond and Mary Ebbet), Stuart Alliance, Islander Alliance, New Life Alliance, Lake Wales Alliance, First Alliance Lakeland, Middleburg Alliance, Christ Cares Alliance, Iglesia Alianza Hialeah, and Spanish First Alliance Orlando (Jojo, Bibi, Eduard, and Pablo Andres), as well as Iglesia Jehova-Jire, Iglesia Punta Gorda, Iglesia Roca Viva, Ft. Lauderdale International Alliance, Hillside Alliance, and Hope Alliance and our sending church, First Alliance Orlando, including Annalena Noble, Dan and Pat Bouw, and Chuck Martinez's Bible Study.

Finally, and most of all, for Gabi and Jon, and our grandson, Elliot—we pray that one day he will read these pages and carry the hope as a child of peace.

Introduction

I'M WRITING FROM INSIDE evangelical life—for everyday believers, for pastors and leaders, and for anyone who wants a clearer story than the standard narrative of Christianity for we all know the power of the stories we live by, and the stories we hold on to.

This is not a Da Vinci Code detour. I am not trafficking in secret documents, "lost gospels," or an alternate Jesus—though I am willing to ask whether some early Jewish memory streams were sidelined as the Church's center of gravity shifted and the Fathers' interpretive authority hardened. More importantly, I'm simply taking seriously the people the Gospels keep placing near Him—Mary, James, Jude, and the first witnesses—and asking what their proximity clarifies.

I'm grateful for historical Jesus research and Second Temple studies that have helped recover Jesus' Jewish world. I draw on that work and share its best instinct: let context do the heavy lifting, even when I cannot follow the skeptical drift that sometimes colors the conclusions. This book asks what we might recover beyond the controversies—family memory, covenant logic, and inside-the-house testimony that the canon itself preserves.

I also introduce a term I learned from a Jewish teacher: Torat Edom—"the teaching of Edom." In Scripture, Edom begins as a brother-story (Jacob and Esau) and becomes a recurring signal for what happens when kinship curdles into rivalry and covenant gets twisted into conquest. Torat Edom functions like a mirror: it helps Christians notice where certainty hardens into contempt, where prophecy becomes a permission slip for spite, and where "winning" replaces faithfulness. It is not a new gospel. It is a diagnostic meant to call us back to covenant order—mercy, truth, and humility.

Because reading correctly requires listening again to Jewish sources—the Hebrew Bible as *Tanakh* Torah, Prophets, Historical scripture (and its ancient translations), Second Temple history and literature, and the interpretive memories preserved in Jewish tradition—not as replacements for the New Testament and not against it, but as essential contexts for hearing it clearly.

I write, too, as a missionary and humanitarian. On the ground, theology cannot remain abstract. You have to answer questions that shape real communities and real wounds:

- What is the gospel?
- What is God doing in history?
- Who is Israel in that story, and where do the nations fit?

This book assumes God has been speaking one coherent word—from creation to new creation—through Israel, through Jesus, and through the witness of His people. If there is confusion, it lies not in God's faithfulness but in our handling of His story: our ease in splitting "Old" and "New" into competing volumes, our habit of framing law and grace as if they belonged to different gods, and our tendency to treat Jesus' Jewish family as a prologue rather than central characters in the covenantal drama.

So rather than offering timelines or predictions, I return to the early witnesses who first lived the story: Jesus' family (Mary, James, Jude), the Nazarene movement (Acts 24:5), the woman at Jacob's well, and Paul's empire-wide testimony. In the healthiest moments of the early movement, these were not rival centers but complementary callings—Jerusalem as the story-keeping hearth and the apostolic mission as outward-going witness.

Why does this matter for "last days" teaching?

"*From his mouth comes a sharp sword . . .* " (Rev. 19:15). The sword is not in His hand. It is from His mouth. The conquering weapon is speech—truth that exposes, judges, and heals. Revelation's Rider is not a permission slip for sacred violence; He rides in righteousness, not in our rage.

I learned to read this passage more carefully from my professor—and friend—Simon J. Kistemaker, who taught Revelation with pastoral clarity. And as someone who honors the Reformed tradition, I note with admiration what Kistemaker did that Calvin did not: he wrote on the Apocalypse, a book Calvin famously left untouched in his commentary corpus.

That matters, because evangelicals have often taken "last days" texts meant to *purify* the Church and used them to *authorize* our image of the Church—certainty at times without humility, zeal without mercy, conviction without trembling. When that happens, we don't just misunderstand prophecy; we misrepresent the King.

Add modern media to that mixture and the danger multiplies. Outrage becomes liturgy, algorithms become catechisms, and Christians can be recruited into fear and tribal belonging without noticing. In that environment, prophecy is easily weaponized into content, and nationalism becomes spiritually futile—promising destiny while reshaping the Church into a tribe with a flag. The nations matter to God, but none can carry the weight of salvation, and none may replace the cruciform shape of discipleship.

Even Isaiah 63—"Who is this who comes from Edom?"—with its startling, blood-red garments (that eerie "red" echo of Esau/Edom) lands best when we hear it for what it is: judgment poetry. It's the LORD confronting oppression, vindicating the afflicted, and settling accounts in the contested neighborhood of Israel's near kin—without anyone's military "help," without any borrowed empire, without any baptizing of violence.

Yes—"He is trampling out the vintage," we sing (or once sang). That line didn't fall out of the sky; it rode Isaiah's winepress imagery straight into an American Civil War hymn. And for someone like me—who loves the old hymns and Classic Rock—that mash-up is part of my bloodstream. But the point isn't to hand Christians a soundtrack for righteous aggression. The point is covenantal reckoning: righteousness and deliverance. God's justice for the crushed. God's rescue for the oppressed.

So no—Isaiah 63 isn't a template for sanctifying bloodshed, contempt, or triumphalism. It's a warning shot against the very instincts that turn covenant into conquest. It's the LORD saying: I will judge. I will save. I will set things right. And He doesn't need our lust for holy war to do it. And yet—mysteriously—He does choose to involve us, because we are His temple, His embodied presence in the world. Our calling is not to mimic the winepress, but to bear witness to the Judge who heals.

That is why "hating Esau"—hating Edom—remains a living biblical warning, not a slogan of reprobation. Edom is not merely an ancient enemy or a map location. It becomes shorthand for the temptation of fratricide: kinship denied, resentment baptized, power justified "in God's name." And if our end-times teaching makes us more violent—even only in tone, in certainty, in contempt—then we have misunderstood the King whose sword is speech, not steel.

What follows is not a new faith, but repentance within the faith: a turning from partial frameworks toward fuller trust in the One who has been faithful all along. Read these pages the way you would sit with relatives around a kitchen table after a funeral—stories overlapping, memories contested, laughter and lament mingled.

Some things will feel familiar. Others may unsettle long-held assumptions. But the aim is simple: to love Jesus more as Israel's Messiah, to honor the authentic Jewish root of the gospel more deeply, and to recover hope without hysteria—learning again to read the Bible as an authoritative library, and to hear how the last words of the Tanakh press us toward repair: the turning of the fathers' hearts to the children, and the children's hearts to the fathers—so that families, and in time the people of God, may be healed and their witness increased.

After many years of study and lived experience, and a long, stubborn striving to make things as simple as possible—not because the realities are simple, but because I have watched too many conversations die in real time: eyes glazing over, attention drifting, good people losing the thread not from lack of sincerity, but because our inherited narratives can be so thick that insight never gets a clear landing. So yes—this is simple in the way a well-told story is simple. But the facts underneath are complex, and the "dots" only begin to make sense when they are connected with patience and honesty.

In fact, a key piece of this book was clarified in conversation early in our home assignment with Sarah and Brian Bennetch—fellow pilgrims in mission, friends with whom we shared places lived and roads walked—when I found myself trying, again, to reassure them (and perhaps myself): I'm going to try to simplify this. Not to flatten it, not to reduce it, but to tell it plainly enough that ordinary disciples can hold it, test it, and talk about it without fear.

That is the spirit of these pages: not a performance, not a new system, but a return—toward clarity, toward family, toward repair, and toward the faithful God who has been speaking all along.

Welcome to the family table. Let's listen again to the story we left behind.

Chapter 1—The Wound and the Witness

> *"When you are arguing against Him (the Jewish Jesus), you are arguing against the very power that makes you able to argue at all: it is like cutting off the branch you are sitting on."*
>
> —C. S. LEWIS, *MERE CHRISTIANITY*[1]

I DIDN'T GROW UP afraid of the Last Days; I grew up certain of them. The world I inherited didn't treat prophecy as a side subject. It was atmosphere in the 1970s—something you breathed. And like most witnesses, I carry wounds, some even self-inflicted. Mine formed where sincere love for Jesus met an end-times story that could slide—almost without noticing—into conquest: the way we talked about Israel, power, and "being on the right side" and ready for the rapture.

I'm the son of German and Eastern European refugees from the Second World War who landed in Cleveland, Ohio. Our world ran on hard work, clarity, and conviction. My Sunday school teachers were serious and steady.

1. C. S. Lewis (1898–1963) and "making room at the table"—Lewis's warning in *Mere Christianity* about "arguing against Him" took on a concrete shape in his later household life. After marrying Joy Davidman, an American writer of Jewish background, Lewis became a widower and stepfather to her two sons. In later reminiscences, Lewis is remembered as taking pains to accommodate Jewish practice in the home for David Gresham—making room at his table for Jewish identity and, where possible, kosher and mitzvah-keeping rhythms—an embodied reminder that the Jesus Christians confess is the Messiah of Israel. See Barnes and Keefe, "Tale of Two Jacks," reporting Lewis's household accommodations for his stepson David Gresham's Orthodox Jewish practice (including kosher-related provisions); on Joy Davidman's Jewish background, see "Romantic and realistic," *Christian History Magazine*, and "The Writings of Joy Davidman Lewis (1915–1960)," *Lewisiana*.

Truth mattered. You could feel it in the room. But so did certainty. Prophecy charts. Rapture films. Israel, Russia, the Middle East, the Antichrist—everything felt like it was lining up. The evening news didn't calm that down; it fed it. And in an immigrant home, "the Jews" weren't distant figures in a Bible lesson. They were part of memory—part of dinner-table conversation—part of the way Europe and the wars still haunted the present.

When I look back, I can see that our certainty wasn't always the same as confidence. Sometimes it was pride—Cleveland pride, the kind that runs deep in a city that has learned to live with long seasons of losing. More often, it was fear. Sometimes it was ignorance dressed in Bible language. We "knew," but we didn't really know.

And as I grew, I noticed a second current in the wider prophecy subculture. Alongside the fascination with the modern State of Israel, there was often an instinct—quiet, sometimes respectable—to blame the Jews, to speak about them with suspicion, even while praising Israel from the pulpit. It wasn't always shouted. It wasn't always named as hatred. But it was there: a tone, a smirk, a loaded aside—an old anti-Jewish reflex hiding inside end-times certainty.

Our refugee community made all this personal. Antisemitism wasn't a topic; it was a wound people carried within my church family. We argued about it precisely because we had seen what ethnic hatred does to human beings—and many in our pews had lived under it as ethnic Germans in lands ruled by other nations and peoples, then escaped it when the political disaster of race-thinking began to collapse under the weight of a war it had started.

One reason observant Judaism drew respect in our world was its visible faithfulness: practiced rhythms, Sabbath rest, reverence—ways of life modernity tries to grind down. We had watched communities survive by living side by side—interacting, sometimes interdependent, learning how to endure without surrendering the texture of their convictions.

And there was another layer: most of us came from free church streams that had learned the hard way what happens when a state church becomes a tool of power. Some of our own ancestors had been harried, fined, or pushed to the margins for refusing imposed religion. So, when we encountered Jewish communities, whose faith was carried not merely in ideas but in embodied obedience and communal memory, it resonated. We recognized something familiar: a people refusing to be flattened.

My Oma remained in Germany and lived into her late nineties. She visited us often. Her sister—Tante Ruth—who immigrated to the U.S. after the war and sponsored my mother and uncle, lived to be 105 and stayed lucid to the end. I can still picture her with popular prophecy publications in hand, turning pages with the same steady attention she gave the morning paper. I loved her as a surrogate Oma—as she was for so many. And I remember her hands: the way she would rub mine, that quiet, steady tenderness—as only a German can love. And I remember the men at our church too, who expressed their love the same way they did everything else: with a firm handshake.

My Oma used to say, "Every generation thinks it's the end"—almost amused, never dismissive. Her sister in America didn't disagree; she simply delighted in the American fascination with "prophecy," the feeling that we might be living at the hinge of history. But even then, I sensed my Oma's reserve. Our end-times excitement was not just spiritual curiosity; it had a uniquely American way of braiding itself to politics—right there in the life of our churches.

Both women told me stories about my great-grandfather, who was a lay preacher. He was licensed to sell chickens to Jews, and they were the delivery girls. He left his work as a baker and returned to farming and lived close enough to Jewish life that he began keeping Sabbath himself. Not as a custom, but as a learned seriousness—a recognition that holiness has a calendar.

And on my father's side there was another kind of proximity. He came from a world he took me back to when it was still Yugoslavia, and it marked me. My father told the stories, and I heard them again from my grandfather—whom I loved to be with—a master tailor who trained apprentices. They spoke of Muslim and Jewish apprentices, not as "others," but as neighbors and coworkers. They shared streets and work and a kind of ordinary understanding.

It wasn't utopia. But it was proof that coexistence isn't a fantasy. It's often what happens when people aren't being organized by fear and politics, yet being Volks Deutsch, the Nazis had a greater influence among them then the Reichs Deutsch world of my mother who perhaps saw the danger.

That formed a reflex in me early: don't toy with hatred. Don't accept stereotypes. They turn real people into props for someone else's resentment. At the same time, don't pretend secular modernity leaves anyone untouched. It doesn't. It pressures every community—Jewish, Christian,

Muslim, and everyone in between. Part of growing honest is learning to tell the difference between contempt and truth: mocking Jews as Jews is poison; naming what modernity does to a people is simply clarity. The tragedy is how quickly outsiders collapse complexity into caricature.

When *The Hiding Place* film hit, the Holocaust stopped being "history." It landed with weight and shook me—and then, strangely, I bolted from the youth group. Looking back, I can name the fault line: you can't play with prophecy when hatred is doing that to real people. What held me—even then—was Presence. Even in my teen years, when I drifted and didn't intentionally follow the Lord, I never had the sense that He drifted from me.

Meanwhile, our immigrant stubbornness showed up in more ordinary ways. Our church was determined to keep the German language alive. My parents spoke it at home and sent me to German school on Saturdays while my friends were out playing or watching cartoons. I was a lousy student, but I loved the old fables—especially *The Bremen Town Musicians*—and I loved the sharp satire of Wilhelm Busch's comics my grandfather read to me in German dialect.[2] And when I failed, I'd sometimes hear the name *Dummer Esel*—"dumb donkey," or in English . . . you know what it means.

All I wanted most back then was to listen to rock bands from the '60s and '70s, vinyl records, album covers you could stare at for hours, lyrics that felt like sacred text. I could sense a kind of longing inside those songs—something that ended and left me hungry for more—but I didn't have words for it yet. I couldn't speak it or write it. I could only turn it up, howl, and jump around.

Later, plenty of Christians became convinced that rock records carried subliminal messages and needed to be burned. Even after I became a Bible-thumper, I felt torn about that. Some music is plainly destructive. Since the 1960s, there has been a soundtrack to a world coming unhinged. But some of it—especially among folk, protest singers and even heavy metal—carried something else: a rough kind of witness. Not clean, often raw. Not catechism-ready, but honest. A cry for justice. A protest. A hunger

2. Wilhelm Busch's (1833–1908) picture-stories look like children's comics, but they bite like satire. In works such as *Max und Moritz*, *Die fromme Helene*, and *Pater Filucius*, Busch turns slapstick cruelty into a mirror of 19th-century German society. The pranks of boys and animals shred the dignity of pastors, teachers, pious widows, and petty bourgeois figures, exposing hypocrisy, harsh child-rearing, and churchly pretension. Behind the singsong rhymes and playful drawings lies a very adult critique of "respectable" morality—anti-clerical, anti-bourgeois complacency, and merciless toward the self-satisfied middle class.

for something true, even when the singer didn't know the name of the One they were reaching for.

Then, in 1981, an Irish band in the middle of the punk era played a club in Cleveland and somehow validated the longing I'd been hearing for years.[3] Before long, they were turning up on a Sunday-morning radio show—slipped in by a DJ alongside Christian rock, even though they weren't part of the usual rotation. Their songs felt disruptive, sometimes apocalyptic laced with biblical imagery, like a prophetic edge smuggled into the soundtrack of my youth. So, when our pastor—who had served in Africa—baptized me after I finally turned to follow the Scriptures I'd long-known in my head, "This gospel shall be preached unto all nations and then the end shall come" and "Go" didn't land as puzzles to solve; they landed as orders.

Looking back, I can see the forces that formed me. As a child of immigrants who loved Jesus, I grew up knowing the world could shift overnight. And through my era's fixation on the Last Days, I came to believe the world was already half-packed for the history bin. Put those together and you don't get calm. You get hunger. You get urgency. You get someone who can be . . . a bit much.

But over time, I learned the center is not a chart, not a countdown, not even the music that woke my heart up. The center is Presence—and He was with me all along, even when I was running in the opposite direction. Such a direction does not permit us to use the Last Days as a hiding place for fear or to let end-times certainty become a respectable cover for contempt—especially toward the very people whose wounds the Church is commanded to honor, not exploit.

Because urgency isn't neutral. It builds something in you. And it builds something in your children. At first, you don't notice. You just call it obedience. You call it sacrifice. You call it "living for eternity." You quote the verses. You mean well. You're not lying when you say you love Jesus. But urgency has a shadow.

3. U2's music carried an apocalyptic honesty that formed many of us before we had words for it. Bono has often said he'd rather be remembered for the music than the activism, yet over time, the activism and the platform became inseparable and he insufferable—and his "moral voice" felt selective and "called out" by other musician like Roger Waters formerly of the rock giant Pink Floyd, who stood for injustice as expressed in their "vintage rock" of the 70s known so well by my generation. U2 finally broke their silence on Gaza and Israel, condemning Hamas's October 7 atrocities while also sharply criticizing Israel's conduct of the war and urging humanitarian access and a political path toward coexistence. Mouriquand, "'Depravity and lawlessness.'"

A Calling That Formed Us as a Family

After being challenged at a Keith Green memorial concert,[4] I left Cleveland and took my machinist work to the engine room of Operation Mobilization's Doulos—a missionary ship. I didn't know what lay ahead. I only knew I had to go. I carried that mix of zeal and naïveté.

Then God did what He often does in mission: my life merged with Gloria's. She was born in Peru but had been a pastor in Brazil, on a real path toward becoming a Methodist bishop, and she walked away from it—forsaking stability, title, and the obvious "career" track—for world missions. But she didn't come to that calling out of a tidy, middle-class religious story.

As children, she and her brothers and sisters found family through a mission-planted Alliance (C&MA) church in Lima. A church became a home. The Gospel became family. That kind of rescue doesn't just shape you; it names you. And still, she chose the harder obedience. Her distant earthly father had other plans, pressing for the respectable future. He saw her intelligence and expected her to become a doctor. Gloria heard all of that, felt the weight of it, and chose an Alliance Bible college in Ecuador instead.

We married in Peru, went on to Prairie Bible College in Canada, had our only daughter there, and raised her in the middle of mission. Ports, storms, languages, cultures, kimchi, and a sense of urgency that never really let us rest. After the *Doulos*, we served on the *Logos II*, including a year on a Korean ship called the *Hannah* in Micronesia. We never really packed or unpacked. We just kept sailing, flying—always moving. And yet, all that left its own baggage.

Learning and Unlearning

On the ships, I met a different kind of Christian—and many coworkers among Muslims who were not shaped by the Christian Zionist instincts of my world. After Bible college, and later in seminary, a fellow student wrote *Dispensationalism: Rightly Dividing the People of God?* That critique helped me see how powerful interpretive systems can be—not only in what they

4. Keith Green and last-days urgency—Keith Green (1953–1982) and his wife, Melody, both from secular Jewish homes, became central voices in the 1970s Jesus music movement through *Last Days Ministries*. Green's call to repentance, justice, and mission shaped a generation, fusing end-times expectation with concrete obedience—care for the poor, evangelism, and a refusal of performative religion. His death in a 1982 plane crash became, for many, part of the wound-and-witness story chapter 1 is naming.

illuminate, but in what they quietly train us to ignore. Over time, it pressed a deeper question: how easily do Christians of many stripes—dispensational, Reformed, and otherwise—end up speaking over Jewish people while debating "Israel" as a concept or a political entity?

A framework can claim to honor Israel and still redefine Israel from the outside. It can also tidy the biblical family tree by fading out other brothers. In many Christian accounts, Ishmael vs. Issac and Esau vs. Jacob become negative space—useful contrasts that keep our categories clean, even when the story of Scripture refuses that kind of neatness.

Reformed clarity brought real strengths, but it often frames the questions more in systematic categories than in story. It also tends to miss the Maccabean world as a necessary prologue to the New Testament—often because those books sit outside the Protestant canon even while their history saturates the Gospels. And it does not always begin where the Gospel began in history: with Jesus' own family—with Mary, James, and Jude—the ones who heard Him first and lived closest to His voice.

Through the years—after the ships, long stretches of travel with a Swedish organization, and seasons of voracious reading—my understanding of eschatology began to steady. R. C. Sproul helped early on with *The Last Days According to Jesus* (my title intentionally echoes his). His tradition gave me something I needed: a disciplined way to read Jesus' words in context—to listen longer and react less quickly.

And yet, I began to sense a limitation in that stream as well. It can treat the destruction of the Second Temple—and Jesus' fulfillment—as such a decisive closure that Israel herself fades from view or become spiritualized, as if the Jewish people are now largely out of the picture in God's ongoing purpose. I couldn't accept that—not biblically and not morally.

Still, it didn't solve everything, but it gave me a starting point I still trust: Jesus Himself speaking in time to real people in Israel's covenant world.

Called Again

As empty nesters—fresh off a season of consulting for other missions and looking back on 15 years when we'd essentially lived in airplanes after the ships—we heard "Go" again. We had served in organizational development for a global children-at-risk work in many countries and even served with R. C. Sproul's Ligonier Ministries on various translation projects.

Then came the call to Italy from the Alliance church in Peru. After a very mobile 25 years, we have now served there for 15—longer than anywhere else. Italy did something to me. Not because it's beautiful (it is), but because it's mixed. It's old. It's layered—deep in history and deep in wounds.

And Christianity isn't the assumed background music the way it can still feel in American evangelical spaces, even if Christian images are everywhere. In Italy, you meet Catholic friends who are nominal. You meet secular neighbors who don't care. You meet Muslim refugees whose lives have been torn open. You meet Latin American migrants cohabitating with Italian atheists. And suddenly, your theology must learn how to inhabit that kind of space.

The pastorate challenged more than any season before it. Our small congregation became a kind of laboratory for mission in a religiously mixed, spiritually calcified world—set in the churn of a busy tourist destination where I deeply interacted with Rome's clergy.

Nearby, I studied in the philosophy faculty of the Pontifical University of St. Thomas Aquinas, concentrating on Thomas and his German brother, Meister Eckhart, and their high scholastic world and thought commonly known as the "Dark Ages."[5] (He's sometimes called a forerunner of German philosophy, which can sound ominous and dark.) And even there I began to detect something—unexpectedly, unmistakably—Jewish in his thought.

Eckhart is known for the verse, "*The Light shines in the darkness, but the darkness cannot overcome the Light*" (see John 1:5) and his use of "abandonment." It may be the closest word for what my family felt at points. Jesus' own family carried a similar tension, and missionary families still do. Yet Eckhart reaches for "abandonment" to name union with Jesus—where the self yields, where control breaks, where Presence is no longer an idea but a life lived. That is why his famous Mary and Martha sermon matters: in his reading of Luke 10:38–42, he dares to praise Martha—not because contemplation is wrong, but because love is proved in a steadied, surrendered active life.[6]

As for family and missions, nothing is neat or tidy. As George Verwer—the late founder of Operation Mobilization—used to say, world missions is messiology. I've been part of that mess, but we have a Messiah who

5. The same Pope John XXII who canonized Thomas Aquinas in 1323 later issued the bull In Agro Dominico (1329), condemning propositions drawn from Meister Eckhart's teaching.

6. Eckhart, "Sermon Nine (Pf 9, Q 86)," 83–90.

gives the potential for restoration. By His very Presence, He gathers what has been scattered—and we will trace such a restoration in chapter 7.

Grief

Then came 2025. During home assignment—while Gloria and I were in Brazil for speaking engagements—I learned from a friend's social media post that my youngest brother was missing. My family searched for him across the city; he was found having taken his own life.

I wasn't there. I was in Brazil, busy with ministry. And I can't pretend that doesn't matter. They called me when he was found. His death tore open an old wound I have carried for decades: the cost of following what I believed was God's leading, and the quiet way that cost is often paid by the ones who stay—the ones who carry the load.

I know the verses for our calling, but grief will not let you hide behind your own words—least of all when you are the oldest son. It asks a question you can't preach away: Who held what I laid down?

I remember the first time I left for the ships. My little brother was 12. He didn't take it well—he cried. I had been close to him, advising him while I was still living at home, and my mother, who didn't shed a tear—East Prussian to the bone—sent me off with the solemn nod reserved for sons going to war. I was leaving for "world missions," but to him—and to his friends at our church's Boys' Brigade, where I was their ride and guide—it felt like a great loss: Marty was gone.

Years later, at our father's funeral, I watched my brother carry what I did not. He cared for our parents. He bore the weight of ordinary faithfulness—the daily, unglamorous labor of presence: appointments, bills, repairs, phone calls, long drives, hard conversations, and the slow attrition of aging. Standing there, I felt the question sharpen: not "Was my calling real?" but "What did my calling cost—especially as the firstborn?"

Throughout my childhood, my father fed my historical and global vision—Civil War battle sites, trips back toward the old country, a house stocked with *National Geographic*. My little brother didn't receive that same kind of attention. But he still absorbed the story and made it his own—only his version turned toward responsibility. He became a successful salesman, and in the end, he cared for both our parents faithfully.

It was my little brother who paid for our father's funeral—simply out of love. My father was often ambivalent about my calling. He never believed I would be there when he passed, but the Lord made it possible in

His perfect time. As Gloria and I had just returned from Peru visiting our family there and to say thank you to the Peruvian Alliance that supported us fully in our first years in Italy. Those days were brief and bruising: we buried my father in the morning and boarded a flight to Sweden that same evening for scheduled Holy Week ministry.

In those short hours together, I noticed a "COEXIST" bumper sticker on my brother's car. It didn't offend me. It clarified something: we had taken different spiritual paths, but we longed for the same peace, the same hope, the same Jesus.

I began writing this book grieving, in part, to honor him—and to tell the truth about the wound mission families often carry: not only what we gave up, but who bore the cost when we were gone.

After Brazil, Gloria and I went on to Peru for the centennial—one hundred years of Alliance missions and the national church. And while we were there, the remembrance service for my little brother took place back home. I stayed with that part of our furlough speaking schedule and to honor Gloria as I watched online. I arrived in Cleveland as a surprise days later to be with my mother, but the damage was already done.

A Family Story—and an Alliance Story

Long before The Alliance called itself an Acts 1:8 family as His global witnesses, A. B. Simpson believed the last days were not a countdown but a call—a summons to global witness shaped by the broken heart of God. His first biographer, A. W. Tozer, carried that prophetic burden into the generation before me, and I devoured his books.

Simpson preached Christ from a distinctly Jewish-shaped gospel long before formal Jewish–Christian dialogue existed. He insisted that God's promises to Israel were central—not merely symbolic—and he publicly condemned antisemitism when others stayed silent. In recent years, the Alliance's former missionary training college campus in Nyack, New York, was sold to a Hasidic Jewish community; Simpson and his wife were still buried there beneath a marked tombstone.

When New York State requested that Simpson's remains be relocated as part of the sale, the Jewish community—despite what one might normally expect under halakhic precedent regarding graves—ensured the move was carried out with dignity, that the burial would remain publicly accessible, and they covered the cost. A century after Simpson prayed for the Jewish people, they honored him. This is not irony. This is covenant.

Our Alliance history is full of courage and sacrifice, but also blind spots, fractures, and unfinished repentance. I cannot resolve all of that either. What I can do is love this movement honestly—grateful for its calling, clear-eyed about its failures—and entrust its story, like my own family, to the One who is faithful in every generation. As The Alliance expanded, the wider evangelical world shifted—revivalism, Bible conferences, culture wars, the prophecy industry.

Urgency hardened into fear and often, chaos. Mission blurred into speculation. Israel became more a political symbol than a covenantal sign. We absorbed anxieties—prophecy updates, Christian nationalism, end-times politics—even as God was drawing the different peoples of the Holy Land and the nations to Himself in astonishing ways. Still, the movement born to unite the nations in *Jesus Only* also struggles with the divisions of the nations.

Returning to Our First Love

So, this book is a window into my own brokenness. It is also a prayer for return—for me, for my family, and for the Alliance family to be an intentional instrument of healing the many divisions in our world. We were formed to stay close to the heart of God: informed by the Jewish world of Jesus, open to the nations, anchored in hope rather than hysteria.

We were never meant to live under fear. We were meant to live as branches—repenting, abiding, witnessing, suffering, loving, believing, sharing, forgiving, persevering, and telling the truth about our own wounds and the world.

The first Alliance gatherings literally called themselves "branches." And *branch* is also the Scriptural word that surrounds the earliest public name for Jesus' followers. The Book of Acts preserves it in a courtroom accusation: "a ringleader of the sect of the Nazōraioi" (Acts 24:5). That label sits in the same family of words that echo through Israel's hope: *Netzer* (*shoot/branch*) and *Notzrim* (*watchmen/keepers*). I didn't arrive at this as a sudden insight or a provocative take. It grew over years—through lived mission and study.

Chapter 2—Why This Generation Distrusts Prophecy Teachers

"I would rather play with the forked lightning or take in my hands living wires with their fiery current, than speak a reckless word against any servant of Christ."

—A. B. Simpson, *Days of Heaven Upon Earth*

"Do not despise prophecies, but test everything; hold fast what is good."

—1 Thessalonians 5:20–21

Before we talk about Jesus' family and their world, this book must tell the truth about the moment we are living in. Something has shifted—quietly at first and now unmistakably. Many in the rising generation do not merely doubt today's prophecy teachers, they distrust them.

That distrust can become cynical or unfair. But it did not come from nowhere. In many cases, it is a response to real damage and real confusion.

This chapter follows one connected chain: how our media environment forms attention and emotion, how that shapes tribal instincts, how tribal instincts harden into nationalist or denominational certainty, and how those dynamics often reach for scapegoats—especially Jews—while reducing Israel to a symbol in our political drama. The result is not only bad theology but damaged people: a generation trained for anxiety, suspicion, and outrage.

The Shadow Over "Prophecy" Right Now

In parts of evangelicalism, a volatile mixture has seeped into the bloodstream: Christian nationalism, prophetic speculation, political absolutism, doom and gloom, and distorted definitions of Israel shaped more by geopolitics than by Scripture.

Put together, this mix doesn't produce courage; it breeds suspicion. It turns believers inward, flattens Scripture into headlines, and hardens people who were meant to grow in holiness and action.

Beneath it all, an older echo rises again whenever we hear talk about "a race" and the easy scapegoating that follows. Sometimes it shows up as open contempt. Sometimes it hides behind "respectable" religious language—less a stated hatred than a reflex: suspicion, caricature, the quiet permission to blame.

Whatever costume it wears, it must be named plainly. Antisemitism is not merely social or political. It is spiritual hostility toward the God who placed His Name on a people and toward the covenant purposes that name announces.

Shem—Noah's son—was named after Somebody. His very name means "name," and Scripture ties the LORD directly to that covenant line: "*Blessed be the LORD, the God of Shem*" (Gen. 9:26). Calling on the Name begins even earlier: "*People began to call upon the name of the LORD*" (Gen. 4:26).

Israel is not first a tribal nickname or a modern political label. It is a new name given to Jacob in a night of wrestling: "You have struggled with God and with humans and have overcome" (Gen. 32:28, NIV). The name *Israel* carries the sense of a people marked by covenantal struggle—disciplined, corrected, sanctified—rather than effortless triumph.

And if Muslim friends hear a striving Jihad echo in this, they're not wrong to notice a family resemblance at the level of words. But Israel's defining struggle, biblically, is never a mandate to baptize violence. It is the sanctifying wrestling of a people bound to the living God—marked by the Name, corrected by the Name, and called to bear the Name.

One reason prophecy talk goes sideways in modern evangelicalism is that we've lost the Jewish world that gives the Bible its operating system. Oskar Skarsaune's wide-angle history is useful here[1]—not because it supplies the covenantal conclusions I will press in this book, but because it

1. Skarsaune, *In the Shadow of the Temple.*

shows how deeply the earliest Jesus-believers remained entangled with Jewish life and argument for centuries and how the popular idea of a clean "parting of the ways" after AD 70 can distort the story. When Christians forget that long overlap, Israel becomes easier to treat as a symbol, a tool, or a proof-text rather than a real people with a real covenant vocation and real wounds.

"Jewishness" and the New Covenant

At the same time, "Jewishness" is not a racial myth or a biological essence. It is covenanting peoplehood—genealogy and memory, halakhic belonging (belonging shaped by lived covenant responsibility), and accountability before God. From the beginning, Israel's story includes outsiders drawn in: the mixed multitude leaving Egypt, Rahab, Ruth, Uriah the Hittite, diaspora communities, righteous Gentiles, and converts across the centuries. Any simplistic definition slips through our fingers. Just read Psalm 87: "*The LORD loves the gates of Zion more than the dwellings of Jacob.*"

Like many missionaries, I was formed by the *Perspectives* reader first published in the early 1980s, and I remain grateful for its insistence that the Bible's mission story begins in the Old Testament. It taught many of us to pay attention to the so-called "missionary psalms," especially Psalm 67 and Psalm 87. But I do not follow every move made inside that anthology. In particular, Walter Kaiser's reading of Israel's "missionary call"—often tethered to Psalm 67—can subtly slide toward an "Israel failed/the church carries the mission" mentality.[2] That drift does not do justice to Israel's covenant vocation, nor to the strange, bracing logic of Psalm 87: Zion's gates are not a staging ground for Israel's replacement, but the place where the LORD names the nations in relation to Zion—welcoming them in without dissolving Israel into a generic "mission principle."

Second Temple history also complicates any purely ethnic account of Israel. In the Hasmonean (Maccabean) period, John Hyrcanus's incorporation of Idumeans (Edomites) was coercive and morally fraught, but it exposes the category: Israel could function as a covenantal body with expandable boundaries—defined by allegiance to Israel's God and Israel's law, not by bloodline alone. Josephus even reports that, after this incorporation, they were "hereafter no other than Jews."[3]

2. Kaiser, "Israel's Missionary Call."

3. Josephus, *Ant.* 13.257–258.

And that is precisely why the New Covenant cannot be treated as a late Christian invention that replaces Israel. Jeremiah already names it inside Israel's own prophetic horizon: not a new god, not a new people, but a renewed covenant fidelity—Torah written on the heart, the knowledge of the LORD deepened, sins forgiven—given to "the house of Israel and the house of Judah" (see Jer. 31:31–34). The Mosaic covenant served, in part, as a national and pedagogical yoke—public, boundary-marking, and capable of coercive administration in a historical nation. Jeremiah's promise is different in texture: inward, Spirit-formed, aimed at repaired covenant life rather than mere border maintenance.

So, it is a category mistake—tragically common in Christian framing—to say Jews are "outside the New Covenant" simply because they do not accept the Church's proposed mechanism for bringing belief to all nations through Jesus of Nazareth. The prophets do not talk that way. They speak of Israel's renewal as Israel's promised future and of the nations being gathered to Israel's God without erasing Israel and its faithful lineages. In Romans 11 terms: the New Covenant is Israel's promised renewal in Messiah, and the nations share in it through union with Israel's Messiah—by grafting, not by takeover. Israel is, first, a qahal and an edah—a summoned assembly and a witnessing community (and yes, the echo with ekklesia matters).

When we confuse politics for covenant or geography for vocation, our eschatology loses its center. That posture trains Christians to treat Jews as scenery: romanticized as a sign, weaponized as a proof-text, or dismissed as an obstacle—rather than honored as the oracle-keepers through whom God gave Torah, prophets, wisdom, and finally Messiah Himself (see Rom. 3:1–2).

Prophecy in an Age of Forked Lightning

Simpson's warning about "forked lightning" lands hard in our own day. Many who love prophecy also love evangelism. They preach the Gospel. They open the Scriptures to others. In that sense, evangelism itself has a prophetic character: it bears witness to what God has said and what He will yet do.

But the Church now speaks inside a media-saturated world of pundits, podcasts, "prophetic" hot takes, and algorithm-driven outrage—where believers are trained to talk about nations and powers with maximum confidence and minimum patience. The result is a kind of borrowed certainty: talking points are repeated faster than they can be tested, and emotional velocity is confused with spiritual discernment.

In that atmosphere, apocalyptic language becomes content, crisis becomes currency, and Israel can be flattened into a symbol inside someone else's storyline rather than honored as a real people with real neighbors and real wounds.

That distortion shows up most painfully in how Christians speak about the modern State of Israel and its neighbors. When theology treats Palestinians and Arab peoples as footnotes—or worse, as obstacles in a prophetic script—it is no longer reading the Bible in covenantal key. It is using the Bible to justify hardness. Prophecy was given to purify the Church, not to excuse contempt; to form a people who speak truth with trembling, not a people who win arguments by volume.[4]

Some critiques of Zionism and Christian Zionism are morally serious: they face real injustices, and the grief over what is happening to Israel's neighbors is not performative—it is daily. But other critiques are little more than rage—less a moral argument than a rejection of a faith practice.

Critiquing policies is not the same as despising a people. What is being resisted here is theological contempt and the prophetic manipulation of Jews—and of their neighbors—for the sake of end-times systems. Christian Zionism also tends to import a racial confusion into the discussion: it often speaks as if "Jew" were a blood category or a political label instead of recognizing the real complexity of Jewish identity—and the halakhic order that historically governed it.

So, this book is not a manifesto for or against any modern state. It is a plea for Christians to stop treating prophecy as a political codebook. The fruit of that habit is confusion. And in that chaos, Simpson's image becomes painfully concrete: careless words—about Israel, about the Church, about Jews, about Palestinians, about the nations—can strike like lightning. If the Church is not careful, it becomes part of the same storm it claims to resist.

The Temptation to Treat Politics as Revelation

A century ago, Karl Barth—and alongside him, his younger colleague Dietrich Bonhoeffer—watched a church learn to speak with the state's voice, and they said, "Nein." Not simply nein to natural theology, and

4. Weber, *On the Road to Armageddon*, 155–186.

certainly not nein to careful theology; not nein to prophecy, but nein to any attempt to treat political destiny, national mythology, or "historical necessity" as revelation.

Bonhoeffer pressed the question of Christian unity and the cost of true discipleship, and in the end, his theology was sealed by witness: he refused to let the Church become a religious mask for state power, and he paid for that refusal with his life.

In the Barmen Declaration (1934), the Confessing Church in emerging Nazi Germany rejected the claim that the church may treat other voices—political programs, national myths, or "historical necessity"—as God's Word. Barth's point wasn't academic; it was pastoral and prophetic: when the church starts quoting the nation with religious certainty, it stops hearing Jesus.

This is one reason the rising generation isn't wrong to distrust modern prophecy culture. They have watched Christians absorb the news cycle like Scripture and then preach it back as certainty—often with Israel, Jews, and the nations turned into props inside someone else's storyline. Barth helps name the category error: current affairs are not new revelation. Christ is Lord; no ideology gets to borrow His authority.[5]

Barth is not a simple hero here—any more than Bonhoeffer is a simple slogan. Bonhoeffer is remembered as a martyr, and rightly so, yet his public courage was already settled in his writings long before his indirect involvement in the plot against Hitler. Resolve was not a late development for him; it was the grain of his life.

Barth's mark on theology, too, is real. But his great strength also carried a blind spot—one that systematic theology can struggle to name: the drive to gather everything into an all-encompassing Christological frame. In his doctrine of election, Barth insists that Jesus Christ is both the electing God and the elected man. The problem is not election as such. The problem is what can be lost when Israel's concrete, historical vocation is dissolved into an abstract universal.

When that happens, Israel's covenant identity becomes easily detachable from Israel's actual life,[6] and the biblical warning carried by Edom is softened into something else entirely. Edom becomes either an unredeemable waste—written off as a mere foil—or a concept so generalized that it

5. Evangelische Kirche in Deutschland, "Theological Declaration of Barmen," Thesis 1 and Thesis 2.

6. Paddison, "Karl Barth's Theological Exegesis of Romans 9–11," 486–488.

no longer bites. But in Scripture, Edom is not a metaphysical trash bin. It is a brother-story turned rival, a mirror held up to covenant people when kinship curdles into contempt and calling becomes conquest. Edom is meant to warn and summon us back to covenant fidelity.

Barth did important work repudiating crude "replacement" theology and insisting that the Church cannot be understood apart from Israel. But the question Torat Edom will not let the Church dodge is sharper: does Israel remain Israel in a way that safeguards her distinct covenantal calling—without being dissolved into an abstract universal "humanity-in-Christ"? That is not an anti-Barth reflex. It is Romans 11 realism: the wild branches are grafted in by mercy; they do not replace the tree. We will return to this in Interlude 3.

Two Generations in the Same Pew

In many churches today, two generations sit side by side—often hearing the same words with two very different nervous systems.

> **The chart generation** who was raised on prophecy charts in Sunday school, *A Thief in the Night*–style anxiety, and the constant sense that history might end at any moment. Headline-watching became a form of discipleship, often braided with patriotism.[7]
>
> **The fallout generation** who inherited the fear and sensationalism (sometimes through *Left Behind* and political sermons) without the interpretive framework. They learned panic before they learned peace. Urgency became anxiety. Many of them are not patriotic in the same way—some are simply tired, wary, and allergic to manipulation.[8]

The preacher quotes Jesus—"watch therefore"—and the room splits quietly. Older saints often hear steadiness: *Stay faithful; He is coming.* Younger listeners often hear alarm: *You will never be safe; the world is a threat,* as our nationalism is as well. Same text. Same pew. Two different interior worlds.

7. Boyer, *When Time Shall Be No More*, 46, 80–112; Sutton, *American Apocalypse*, 16–19, 26–28.

8. Frykholm, *Rapture Culture*, 3–5, 8–11, 13.

Deconstructing Fear Is Not the Same as Deconstructing Faith

Most deconstruction is not rebellion. Many younger Christians are not rejecting Scripture or tradition; they are rejecting fear-based Christianity—or perhaps reduced interpretations. Their questions often rise from wounds, not cynicism. They want Jesus without anxiety. Jesus without politics masquerading as prophecy. Jesus without pressure replacing peace.

In North America and Europe, religious disaffiliation is real, and the reasons are complex. Through the last 40 years. there are many people I have spoken with; the first fracture is not Jesus, it is fear-laced religion or dogmatic division.

Many never realized how deeply fear—or pride in certainty—shaped them. Urgency was assumed to be obedience.

When the LORD asks Cain, "Why are you angry, and why has your face fallen?" (Gen. 4:6–7), He names a pattern that repeats wherever worship collapses into rivalry and anxiety hardens into fate. Modern evangelical eschatology can become spiritually dangerous—not because it speaks of judgment (Scripture does), but because it can baptize a Cain-mechanism inside religious people: doctrinal certainty becomes a form of self-justification, and the future becomes a mirror in which the soul rehearses its wounds instead of receiving healing.

That mechanism can activate four destructive emotions at once:

- Guilt—"What if I'm wrong?" so the response is increased dogmatism rather than humility.
- Shame—"What if I lose face?" so certainty hardens—and even the "iron rod" of Christ can become a fantasy of emotional vindication of perceived enemies we should love.
- Fear—"What if I'm not ready?" so readiness becomes panic management or losing an argument instead of faithful presence with repentance.
- Hardness—cynicism and exhaustion because anxious end-times systems and a focus on dogmatism cannot sustain love for actual neighbors; they subtly sustain the outrage at those imagined enemies.

So, the fallen face returns—only now wrapped in prophecy charts and confident tones, even rationally justified. The tragedy is that this is the opposite of what biblical apocalypse is meant to do. Apocalyptic Scripture, read rightly, forms endurance. It unmasks beastly power so the saints can refuse it. It trains the Church to suffer without becoming cruel, to wait without becoming frantic, to witness without needing control.

And the pattern is not unique to Christians. As many evangelicals were raised on Antichrist charts, many Muslims today are raised on end-times narratives about Dajjāl. Fear can counterfeit vigilance in any tradition. Many young believers resist this, not because they reject faith, but because they want to heal, build community, and live what Scripture calls "good news." They ask, "If the Gospel is good news, why does it feel like bad news?" And they are not wrong to ask it.

This book begins with healing. It begins by naming how political absolutism, panic, war, and religious pressure have distorted Jesus' words and reshaped Christian homes. To untangle this, the Church must listen again, closely, to those closest to Him:

- His mother
- His brothers
- His family
- His earliest Jewish disciples

They remind the Church that Christian hope is not a countdown but a character-forming relationship. Much of what was learned wasn't wrong because it was unbiblical. It was wrong because it was anxious or a diversion.

Why the Church Needs Jesus' Family

Before written Gospels, the early community had something else: the family who remembered Him. Mary, James, and Jude—the bearers of the oral Evangelion—handed down not systems but memory. They give posture, not panic; perseverance, not paranoia. Their world was turbulent—Roman brutality, Temple politics, messianic impostors, persecution—yet their voice is steady, gentle, and fearless.

Before speaking of Jesus' mother and brothers, it helps to remember that the first prophetic voice in the Jesus story is not a platformed teacher with a timeline. It is a relative. Luke tells us Mary and Elizabeth are kin (Luke 1:36). John the Baptist does not appear as a detached religious commentator; he rises from a covenant household world—priestly memory, interwoven families, songs, and promises.

And John's central act is not prediction; it is witness: "*Behold, the Lamb of God*" (John 1:29). He points away from himself, away from adrenaline, away from speculative drama, and toward a Person. He decreases, Jesus increases. John's greatness is not celebrity certainty; it is faithful forerunning.

He does not build a brand. He does not monetize certainty. He does not baptize politics as destiny. He steps into the wilderness and says the message that always makes religious crowds nervous: repent. And when power arrives, he does what prophets do: he names the truth even when it costs him his life (see Mark 6:17–29).

This is why the rising generation is not wrong to be cautious. Many have encountered a version of prophetic ministry that cannot decrease—must always be first, loudest, most certain, most urgent. John the Baptist is the corrective.

A Better Way to Read the Last Days

This book offers no predictions. Instead, it returns to Jesus' Jewish world, His family's memory, and a healed eschatology—steady, relational hope. Jesus' final sermon becomes what it always was:

- a compass, not a countdown
- a reassurance, not a threat
- a call to presence, not panic

So, this book is for believers exhausted by fear-based Christianity; for parents walking with deconstructing children; for pastors shepherding polarized congregations; for missionaries engaging Judaism and Islam; for skeptics who still love Jesus; for disciples longing for clarity without panic.

It begins where the earliest disciples were forced to begin—close to the family: Mary's song, James' steadiness, Jude's fierce clarity, and the early Netzarim/Notzrim who kept faith alive after the Temple fell.

And it begins with Jesus—still saying what He always says into storms: "*Do not be afraid.*" The lane taken here is simple: take Matthew 24 seriously in its first-century setting, keep the Bible's covenant patterns in view, and still hold the future hope Israel has always carried—resurrection, judgment, and renewal—without turning the text into either nostalgia or a news-cycle codebook.

This is the last days according to Jesus and His family. And their voice is the one the Church needs now. Let's listen.

Chapter 3—Mary: The Bridge of Mercy

"He has helped His servant Israel, in remembrance of His mercy."

—LUKE 1:54

"And Mary treasured all these things, pondering them in her heart."

—LUKE 2:19

"Mary is the most erased women in history."

—JAMES D. TABOR[1]

MOST CHRISTIANS THINK THEY already know Mary. We know the creche and the carols. Some of us know the controversies. But we rarely meet Mary as she stands inside the story: a first-century Jewish woman at the crossroads of the Abrahamic families, the mother of Messiah whose voice becomes the first sound of the Last Days, and a quiet bridge through whom nations still encounter Jesus.

Historical Jesus scholarship helped me return to her in that way—especially after years living in Italy, where Mary is everywhere, often as an icon detached from her Jewish world. More recently, historian James Tabor has pressed the question in a bracingly historical key, urging readers to see Mary not merely as a devotional symbol but as a real figure of courage and agency within Jesus' family and the earliest Jesus movement.[2]

1. Tabor, *Lost Mary*, 14.
2. Tabor, *Lost Mary*, 13–23.

Whether one shares all his conclusions or not, that insistence is clarifying: Mary belongs first to Israel's story. And when we put her back there, she becomes harder to sentimentalize and easier to hear.

To meet her there, two truths must be held together. Historically, the Judaism of Mary's world was not a single, uniform system. It was contested, layered, and locally embodied—what scholars often call "many Judaisms" (that is, conflicting stories lived in varied communities and settings). That sociological description can be useful, but it should not be treated as a "religions-evolve" authority that the German Higher Critics set into motion over revelation and mission, as if covenant were merely the by-product of religious development.

Jacob Neusner's documentary approach helped clarify the complexity: different Jewish corpora and communities speak in different registers, shaped by different pressures, and later texts cannot simply be treated as transparent reports of "what everyone believed" in the first century.[3]

Yet that complexity does not cancel the unity of God's revelation. "Many Judaisms" does not mean many gods or many competing truths; it names one covenantal story being lived, guarded, argued, and carried forward through real communities under empire. Mary stands inside that one revelation—formed by Israel's prayers and Scriptures, not floating above history as a timeless icon.

At this point, a methodological distinction matters. Much critical historical Jesus scholarship is intentionally disciplined to historical explanation—sources, plausibility, social location—rather than theological claims about revelation. That discipline can be illuminating; it can clear away lazy harmonizations and force us to read texts in their world. But its very method also brackets the category that confessional readers treat as basic: divine self-disclosure. When you rule revelation out in advance, you may still describe Jesus' impact, but you cannot finally account for why Israel's Scriptures speak as they do, why the witnesses speak as they do, or why the earliest communities risked everything to testify. So, we can learn from the historical discipline, but we must not let its self-imposed limits become a metaphysical verdict. We must go where the texts themselves go: to the claim that God has acted and spoken.

Neusner's long debate with E. P. Sanders (founder of The New Perspective(s) on Paul) further exposes a deeper difference in how Judaism is imagined. Much modern scholarship treats religion like a paper trail,

3. Neusner, *Documentary Foundation of Rabbinic Culture*, 1–46.

often without meaning to: doctrines, texts, and reconstructable systems. Neusner keeps pressing a different point: Judaism is a disciplined culture of transmission, where texts often arise to serve a living orality rather than replace it. This does not make the tradition immune to distortion, and it does not make every later source transparent for the first century. But it does mean Jewish continuity cannot be reduced to "late evidence" or to a string of academic reconstructions.[4]

The same caution matters when handling Talmudic material and even when comparing Mary's portrayal in Luke with the Qur'an. We are not only comparing documents; we are comparing communities of memory, debate, and worship. Sanders helped many Christians recover the Jewish matrix of Paul and the early Jesus movement, even if the New Perspective debates that followed sometimes hardened into divisive intramural disputes and even if some trajectories drift toward a developmental account that treats covenant as little more than religious evolution. Neusner's reminder is both methodological and moral: the Jewish matrix is not merely a set of data points but a received tradition with disciplined modes of transmission. And when turning to Paul in the imperial world, one must attend to Rome's governance, synagogue realities, and local patterns of tolerance rather than assuming tidy, one-size-fits-all labels—whether "religio licita" or "covenantal nomism"—can do the historical work for us.[5]

Neusner's point matters for Mary because she is not merely background to Jesus nor a later devotional symbol (as Tabor's book itself forces us to admit). She is a Jewish woman formed inside a living covenant tradition—Scripture as prayed, remembered, and transmitted in the life of Israel. That is why, when she finally speaks, she does not improvise a new spirituality; she gives voice to Israel's inherited hope.

Mary is not the beginning of Christian confusion; she is the beginning of Christian clarity through being Jewish. And in an age of division and fear, it is Mary—more than almost any other figure—who models the path toward humility, unity, and mission. In her, Jews can recognize a daughter of Zion. Christians recognize the mother of their Lord. Muslims honor Maryam as the most revered woman in their scripture. In Mary, the children of Abraham still find a shared doorway through which to approach the God of mercy.

4. Neusner, *Documentary Foundation of Rabbinic Culture*, 179–207.

5. Neusner, *Documentary Foundation of Rabbinic Culture*, 5–13, description, analysis, interpretation.

Yet the way Mary appears in the Qur'an is instructively different from the way she appears in Luke—and this, too, reinforces Neusner's point about communities of memory. In Sūrat Maryam,[6] Maryam (Mary) is largely silent: we hear her fear, her lament, and then her vow of silence. The hymnic energy is carried not by Mary's song but by the narrative itself—and by the child's speech in the cradle.

The Qur'an is a later and different record than the New Testament—another community of memory rather than first-century Gospel testimony—yet its portrayal is still instructive for dialogue because it shows how Mary's name remains a doorway and how Jesus is framed on the other side of that doorway. That contrast helps Luke come into focus: Mary's Magnificat is not a decorative ornament in the Christmas story; it is theologically deliberate.

To understand Mary rightly, she must be returned to the world she lived in. She was not a medieval statue or a Renaissance ideal. She was a young Jewish woman in an occupied land and from a city with a negative reputation—formed by Israel's prayers, immersed in a story older than empire, trained in the vocabulary of covenant. When Mary speaks in Luke, she does not invent a new spirituality; she sings Israel's old hope. The Magnificat is not a sentimental lullaby. It is a prophetic declaration that the God of Abraham is moving again, remembering His covenant, reversing the world's proud hierarchies, lifting the lowly by mercy.[7] Mary's song is the doorway into the Last Days.

Mary's Song of Praise: The Magnificat

Luke 1:46–55:

> 46 And Mary said,
> "My soul magnifies the Lord,
> 47 and my spirit rejoices in God my Savior,
> 48 for he has looked on the humble estate of his servant.
> For behold, from now on all generations will call me blessed;
> 49 for he who is mighty has done great things for me,
> and holy is his name.
> 50 And his mercy is for those who fear him

6. Q 19:16–36 (Saint Murad).
7. Green, *Gospel of Luke*, 97–104.

from generation to generation.
51 He has shown strength with his arm;
he has scattered the proud in the thoughts of their hearts;
52 he has brought down the mighty from their thrones
and exalted those of humble estate;
53 he has filled the hungry with good things,
and the rich he has sent away empty.
54 He has helped his servant Israel,
in remembrance of his mercy,
55 as he spoke to our fathers,
to Abraham and to his offspring forever."

A Bridge Inside the Church

When I lived in Rome, surrounded by priests and religious who had prayed the Rosary since childhood, I discovered something surprising: Mary could open conversations I could not open on my own. I was an evangelical searching for a Jewish-shaped Gospel; they were Catholics shaped by centuries of Marian devotion. Yet when we sat together and opened the Gospels, the room softened. No one felt the need to win. The textual Mary disarmed us.

Her single, crystalline line at Cana—"*Do whatever He tells you*"—became the center (John 2:5). Mary was not a rival to Jesus but a witness to Him: the one who stepped back so He could step forward. Her posture held us in place long enough to listen.

A Bridge Beyond Christianity's Comfort Zones

Mary's bridge-building capacity is even more visible in Muslim–Christian encounter. Many Christians do not realize how deeply Maryam is honored in Islam. Sūrat Maryam presents her as chosen, faithful, and pure. Muslim families name daughters for her, and in many settings, Mary is the safest place to begin a real conversation. I have watched walls come down when Mary enters the room because she is familiar, beloved, and not treated as a provocation. And once Mary opens the doorway, Jesus Himself can step through.

But what steps through that doorway matters. In many Western imaginations, Islam's Jesus is treated as little more than a revered messenger—a moral teacher with miracles attached. Yet the Qur'an's own framing is more textured than that. It repeatedly identifies him as ʿĪsā ibn Maryam—Jesus, son of Mary—and places Him within categories of revelation, guidance, and communal accountability.[8] In other words, the Qur'anic portrait does not merely preserve admiration for Jesus, it preserves a logic and direction of peoplehood. Hold that thought. It carries us next into Interlude 1—Behold Your Mother.

Rabbi Ben Abrahamson has helpfully emphasized this often-missed point: the Qur'an—and the *tafsīr* commentary tradition—presents Jesus not only as a wonder-working prophet, but as a law-bearing figure whose mission gathers and orders a recognizable community marked by the table and love in action, "the people of the table," with real obligations under God. For now, note the shape of that claim for it is the title of his recent book on *Original Christianity*; we will return to it in chapter 9.[9]

Why Mary Matters for the Last Days

In an age shaped by crisis, speculation, and spiritual panic, Mary restores the tone. The Last Days begin with mercy, not fear. They begin with God remembering covenant, not discarding it. They begin with praise that becomes courage. Mary's greatness is her transparency. Protestants need not fear her; Catholics need not place her beyond Scripture. She stands quietly between extremes. Her authority is humility; her glory is obedience; and her entire ministry can be summarized in one sentence: "*Do whatever He tells you.*"

So, in an anxious age, Mary calls us back to the beginning—not merely to the manger, but to the God who "*remembers mercy.*" She bridges what history has divided. She points every Abrahamic conversation toward Jesus. And she teaches us that in the Last Days, the people of God are formed not by panic, but by praise.

Mary is the first disciple in the story Luke tells. She is Israel's daughter who carries Israel's hope. She is the woman Muslims still honor. And she remains, so often, quietly present without drawing attention to herself. As

8. Q 3:50; 5:46–48 (Saint Murad).

9. Abrahamson, "Jesus (ʿĪsā b. Maryam) as Law-Bearer and Community Founder in the Qur'ān and Classical Tafsīr," in *People of the Table.*

James Tabor puts it, Mary is "the best known, least known" woman in history—famous in symbol, often missing in substance.[10] I have focused on the historian's observation, but it also sets our direction: when Mary is restored to her Jewish world, her witness becomes clearer for Jews, Christians, and Muslims alike—and it opens naturally onto what follows.

10. Tabor, *Lost Mary*, 13, 188.

Interlude 1—Behold Your Mother

"But the Jerusalem above is free, and she is our mother."

—Galatians 4:26

I'm reading Mary the way the Bible reads her: inside Israel's covenant story, where "mother" names Zion before it ever becomes a system. This interlude is both a provocation and a deeper dive. It traces Mary into Paul's "Jerusalem above" and Revelation's woman—not to enthrone her, but to let the cross disclose what "mother" means in the economy of promise. Mary is a real daughter of Zion in history, and precisely as such, she functions as a signpost toward the covenant home Christ's blood secures.

At the cross—"in that hour," with blood and water flowing and the world's violence exposed—Jesus says to the beloved disciple, "Behold your mother," and to Mary, "Woman, behold, your son" (John 19:26–27). The Church has argued over that line for centuries. Some hear tenderness. Others tense up, because the words have been claimed by competing systems. But Paul gives us a discipline for moments like this: the meaning of the cross is not captured by the world's categories; it is unveiled by the Spirit (see 1 Cor. 2). That matters here. "Behold your mother" is not an empire-safe sentiment or a denominational proof-text. It is a cruciform disclosure—understood only beneath the cross—where the wound becomes the doorway and covenant belonging is reconstituted in blood.

This interlude is not here to recruit anyone into a Marian system. It is here to refuse every system—Catholic, Orthodox, or Protestant—that tries to domesticate the cross into something manageable. The question isn't, "How high can Mary be lifted?" but "What is Jesus unveiling at the very moment the covenant is being cut—covenant made and sealed through sacrifice, in the deep biblical sense of covenant-making?" Mary does not compete with Christ. She points—through Him—to the home His blood secures.

A brief clarification is needed. Many readers will have encountered popular Catholic treatments that treat John 19 as a direct charter for a developed Marian ecclesiology and devotional program. I'm not writing to adjudicate every claim in that argument here; I'm simply saying plainly: I do not find those readings adequate to the textual and covenantal architecture in view.[1] The cross must set the meaning—not later machinery, even when it speaks in biblical accents.

Mary, Zion, and the Corporate Woman

Catholic Marian arguments often take John 19:26–27 as a direct warrant for Mary's universal motherhood: the beloved disciple represents every disciple, and Revelation 12:17 is then read as confirmation that the mother of the Messiah is also the mother of all believers. That reading has rhetorical power. But it also risks collapsing a covenant symbol into a devotional conclusion.

In Revelation, the woman is first a corporate sign—Zion in travail, the people of promise brought through conflict—within which Mary stands as the most concrete daughter of Zion, not as the sign's whole meaning. Mary is inside the sign as history; she is not the sign's entire referent. Revelation itself signals how we should read the woman: she is crowned with "twelve stars" (Rev. 12:1)—Israel's family sign—she labors to bring forth the Messiah (Rev. 12:2, 5), and then the conflict widens. When the dragon cannot destroy the Child, he turns "to make war on the rest of her offspring" (Rev. 12:17)—defined as those "*who keep the commandments of God and hold to the testimony of Jesus.*" That is covenant language: a faithful people, preserved under pressure, marked by obedience and witness.

I'll return to the "stars" more fully in the chapter on Jude. For now, the key point is simple: Revelation hands us a covenant symbol before it hands us a devotional program. The woman is Zion's mother imagery—the people of promise brought through conflict, preserved in the wilderness, opposed by the dragon, yet carried through by God's keeping (Rev. 12:7–17). Read

1. Pitre, *Jesus and the Jewish Roots of Mary*, esp. the introduction and early chapters, where typology and "Ancient Judaism" are used as interpretive context for how he reads Catholic Marian doctrine.

carefully: Revelation is not giving us a portrait to weaponize or for predictions. It is teaching the saints how to endure without becoming beast-like—how to conquer "*by the blood of the Lamb and by the word of their testimony*," even when the powers rage (Rev. 12:11).

The Mother Jesus Gives Is a Mother-City

Paul states the larger reality in one clear sentence: "*The Jerusalem above is free, and she is our mother*" (Gal. 4:26). That line is not a soft metaphor. It is covenantal architecture. Paul is not inventing poetry; he is naming a reality Israel already knew: the gathered people of God is not first an institution but a mothered people—formed by promise, not force.

The "mother" is not an empire-church, not a private spirituality, and not a floating abstraction. It is the people brought forth by promise rather than coercion—Sarah's barren womb expanded into a city-wide birth. Isaiah shocks us with it: Zion gives birth "in a day" (see Isa. 66:7–13). Hebrews names it with temple realism: "*You have come to Mount Zion . . . the heavenly Jerusalem*" (see Heb. 12:22–24). Revelation completes the picture: the holy city comes down as bride (see Rev. 21–22). So, when Jesus says, "*Behold your mother*," He is not detouring from the cross. He is speaking from inside the wound—disclosing the covenant home being born through His suffering.

The Woman at Cana and the Woman at the Cross

In John's Gospel, Mary appears at two hinges of the story—Cana and Golgotha—and in both scenes, Jesus addresses her as "*Woman*" (see John 2, 19). That is not coldness. It is biblical framing. John is reaching behind our church fights to Eden-language—to the first promise, the serpent, and the seed (see Gen. 3:15).

At Cana, the woman stands at the threshold of new creation as water becomes wine. At Golgotha, the woman stands at the threshold of new covenant life as blood and water flow from the pierced side. John binds the scenes with the language of the "hour": "*My hour has not yet come*" (John 2:4), and "*from that hour . . .*" (John 19:27). Provision for His mother is real. But John is telling us it is never only that. It is covenantal unveiling.

"Behold Your Mother" and Our Modern Reflexes

"*Behold your mother*" forces honesty. It reveals how quickly we get triggered into systems: Roman Catholic excess, Orthodox iconography, Protestant suspicion—maybe even old memories of anti-Catholic zeal that once felt like faithfulness. If that line made you tighten up, you're not alone—and you don't have to pretend it didn't.

But the deeper issue is not only Catholic vs. Protestant vs. Orthodox. It is also part of the modern striving about our witness to the nations. Many of us are recovering "we" again: covenant, Kingdom, community, embodied discipleship. That recovery is often healthy. Yet it has a danger: sometimes, in gaining communal language, we quietly lose the wound—the sheer depth of what the cross is doing for sinners—so that the cross becomes the badge of a renewed community rather than the place where God deals with sin and purchases mercy through blood.

One old contrast can name the tension. Bunyan's *Pilgrim's Progress* gave Protestants a blazing picture of the Celestial City—but in the way many of us received it, the journey can feel like one anxious soul carrying a private burden toward a private escape. Chaucer's *Canterbury Tales*, by contrast, is pilgrimage as a crowded road: classes, contradictions, wounded people, jokes, hypocrisies, and shared motion—community in transit. Neither picture is the whole truth by itself. Bunyan guards personal repentance and faith; Chaucer exposes how inescapably social our discipleship is. Taken together, they illuminate our moment: recovering "we" is good, yet we must not recover "we" in a way that dulls the wound.

That modern dilemma helps explain why current debates about Paul and justification have felt so charged. N. T. Wright (often heard as a leading voice in "The New Perspective(s) on Paul") helps many readers hear the Gospel in its big-Bible register: Israel, covenant, Kingdom, the formation of a people—not only "me and my salvation." That hunger is real. But Wright draws fire from two opposite directions, and both critiques expose something we cannot afford to ignore.

On one side, Messianic Jewish theologians (not least Mark Kinzer) press the question Wright's framework keeps reopening: Does Israel—genealogical Israel—remain Israel in any enduring way, or does Israel get universalized so broadly that Israel's distinctive covenantal calling quietly fades? That tension surfaced publicly in their debate on "the meaning of Israel," framed in blunt questions: Are non-Messianic Jews members of God's covenanted people, and if so, do they as a people retain a unique covenantal vocation?[2] I would press the question further, and I will keep pressing it across these chapters: What becomes of genealogical Israel's ongoing vocation as the "oracle-keepers," the people entrusted with the words of God (see Rom. 3:2)?

On the other side, Wright—and a younger generation of New Testament voices such as Matthew Bates—has been criticized sharply by Reformed Protestants.[3] That criticism is not merely an attempt to shrink the story back down to private religion. It is driven by a fear that certain formulations can dull the wound at the center: the cross as the place where God truly deals with sin and where the verdict of righteousness is not merely a badge of covenant membership or allegiance but a costly divine act secured through blood. That is why major critiques continue to appear, sometimes treating the question as nothing less than the integrity of the Gospel that Wright and Bates both intend to defend.[4]

Why bring that dispute into a Marian interlude? Because it names our contemporary fault line with clarity. We want a collective Gospel again, but we do not want a collective Gospel that quietly dissolves Israel or spiritualizes into replacement abstraction, and we do not want a covenant story so big that the cross becomes a symbol of identity rather than the place where mercy is purchased through blood.

Now bring that same honesty back to the words that divide the Church even faster than N. T. Wright ever will: "*Behold your mother.*" Read in the light of the crucifixion, the "mother" Jesus gives is not a rival queen hovering above the Church. It is a signpost pointing to the covenant home being born through His suffering—the Jerusalem above, the city of promise, the people made free. In that light, "*Behold your mother*" is not a Marian-cult formula. It is a cruciform invitation: recognize your citizenship. The cross is where the mother-city is disclosed—not as empire, but as covenant.

The Beloved Disciple

Some readers have noticed that the only person explicitly called "*the one Jesus loved*" before the Last Supper is Lazarus (see John 11) and have suggested that the beloved disciple may be Lazarus—or that Lazarus at least functions as an emblem of resurrection-witness in John.

2. Wright and Kinzer, "Debate on the Meaning of Israel."
3. Bates, *Beyond the Salvation Wars.*
4. Mohler, "Have We Really Misunderstood the Gospel for 2,000 Years?"

I wouldn't make it a hill to die on. But it does reinforce the central point: at the cross, Jesus is gathering a resurrection-formed community, not merely arranging private care. Whether the beloved disciple is John son of Zebedee, Lazarus, a Johannine witness figure, or (as James Tabor argues) even James, the function is consistent: the beloved disciple stands as representative disciple, receiving the mother into the household of the new creation.

True and False Stars

There is one more thread I can only point to here because it belongs more fully with Jude and the section on Antichrist: Scripture's contrast between true and false lights—between the "*morning star*" promised to the faithful and the "*wandering stars*" that mark counterfeit teachers (see Rev. 2:26–28; Jude 12–13). The true mother-city is anchored, the counterfeit drifts.

That contrast helps us read Paul's "mother" language with depth. In Galatians 4, Paul is not dabbling in symbolism for its own sake; he is locating the people of God inside the Bible's barren-womb logic of promise—life given where life cannot be manufactured. Sarah's story is the shock at the center of Israel's beginnings: the covenant people do not originate in human strength or religious machinery, but in sheer divine fidelity—God bringing fruit out of barrenness (see Gen. 18:10–14; 21:1–3). That theme runs through Scripture like a bright thread: Hannah's song, born from a closed womb, becomes a template for the reversal language Mary will later sing (see 1 Sam. 1–2; Luke 1:46–55). God delights to build His future in places where we have no leverage so that the result is mercy, not boasting.

Paul draws that same covenant logic into his pastoral crisis in Galatia. He contrasts Hagar and Sarah, and he names Hagar's line with "Mount Sinai" (see Gal. 4:24–25)—not because Sinai was evil, but because a good covenant administration can be misused when it becomes the controlling framework for belonging: public, boundary-marking, and—when handled in the flesh—capable of coercion. Paul is warning against a way of constructing identity that must always be enforced, always measured, always secured by visible control.

Sarah, by contrast, represents the mother-city "*from above*," the community born from promise, not pressure: "*The Jerusalem above is free, and she is our mother*" (Gal. 4:26). She is "free" because her children are born by gift—by the Word of promise—rather than by religious manufacture or nominal identity (see Gal. 4:28). That is what makes her anchored.

And here a necessary guardrail must be stated plainly: none of this negates Ishmael. Paul is not rewriting Genesis into an ethnic hierarchy or treating Hagar and her son as disposable. Scripture itself goes out of its way to show the LORD's attention to Hagar: God meets her in affliction, names what is happening, and is not embarrassed to be known as the God who sees (see Gen. 16:7–13). God explicitly blesses Ishmael with real posterity and mercy (see Gen. 17:20; 21:17–21). Paul's point in Galatians 4 is not that Ishmael is outside God's care; it is that covenant inheritance comes by promise rather than by the flesh—and that Gentile inclusion must be received as gift, not seized as entitlement (see Gal. 4:23, 28–31; cf. Rom. 11:17–24). The moment Gentiles or Jews turn promise into possession; they stop being grafted-in branches and start acting like owners. That drift is what Jude will name later—false lights that cannot abide because they do not live by promise.[5]

The Arc

So, the line runs like this:

- **Genesis 3:15**—The woman and her seed; serpent and promise. The first prophecy is not a chart but a wound and a hope: enmity, conflict, a promised victory that will come through embodied history—through covenant faithfulness.
- **John**—The woman at Cana and at the cross; the "hour" revealed. At Cana, the hour is anticipated; at Golgotha, the hour arrives. The woman stands at the opening and the climax where the new creation begins and where it is purchased.
- **Paul**—The Jerusalem above, "our mother," confessed as covenant reality. Paul does not collapse Israel into abstraction; he names a real

5. Paul signals that he is reading the Hagar–Sarah story as an allegorical construal ("these things are being taken figuratively/allegorized," Gal. 4:24), which many scholars treat as midrash-like—not because Paul is quoting later rabbinic midrash, but because he is doing a Jewish, text-saturated rereading that draws covenant identity from the Torah's own internal patterns. For discussion, see Hays, *Echoes of Scripture in the Letters of Paul*; Stanley, *Paul and the Language of Scripture*; Longenecker, *Biblical Exegesis in the Apostolic Period*; compare also Yael Fisch on "midrash-pesher" as a shared Second Temple interpretive technique.

heavenly polity—the mother-city of the faithful—over against every earthly system that tries to manufacture identity by coercion.

- **Isaiah 66/Hebrews 12**—Zion births a people; the heavenly Jerusalem is approached as our true home. We "come to" that Jerusalem now—not by flight from Earth, but by worship, by covenant belonging, by being made into living stones building his human temple prepared for the new one.
- **Revelation 12/21–22**—The woman in travail and the bride-city descending: one people, preserved and then unveiled. The woman's travail and the city's descent are not two stories, but one story told from two angles: the people of God guarded through trial, and then revealed as the bride—glorious, healed, and home.

Mary stands at the crossroads of all of this—not as a rival to Christ, but as a real daughter of Zion who receives the Word, bears the Word, and stands inside the community shaped by that Word. She is not the destination. She is a first witness and a signpost.

And that is why this belongs in a Last Days book. Because it drags readers away from reactive theologies of division—Isaac vs. Ishmael, Jacob vs. Esau, Israel vs. Church, Jew vs. Gentile, spirit vs. body, heaven vs. Earth—and plants us where Jesus planted the beloved disciple: beneath the cross, looking up at the mother-city we did not build. There, the future is not a weapon. It is a home.

Chapter 4—James: The Habits That Hold Us

"Be doers of the word, and not hearers only."

—JAMES 1:22

"Show me your faith apart from your works, and I will show you my faith by my works."

—JAMES 2:18

"The wisdom from above is first pure, then peaceable, gentle, open to reason, full of mercy."

—JAMES 3:17

IF MARY GIVES US the tone of Christian hope, James gives us the texture. Mary sings God's mercy as the dawn of the Last Days. James teaches us what that mercy looks like when it puts on shoes, walks into a meeting, sits at a table, and holds a family together. Mary frames the story. James shows us how to inhabit it.

Why James Gets Misread

In almost every generation, Christians have misunderstood James. Martin Luther, shaped by his own spiritual battles and the weight of medieval penance, once called James "an epistle of straw"[1]—not because he despised James, but because he could not yet see him inside the world James lived in. The Reformation rediscovered Paul but often lost James in the process. What Paul fought in Romans—legalism, boasting, covenant boundary-markers—was simply not what James was addressing in Jerusalem.

Paul was planting missions among Gentiles under empire; James was guarding a fragile community of Jewish believers in a city teetering on the edge of revolt. Their callings were different, their contexts were different, and their emphases were different. But both were servants of the same Lord.[2] When we return James to his Jewish world—what I call the Torat Edom lens, and what Mark Nanos helps illuminate—the picture changes. James ceases to be the "balance" to Paul or the "corrective" to Paul. He becomes the older brother in the family, teaching us how to remain faithful when the world fractures under empire.[3]

Jerusalem and the Weight of Continuity

James was not simply Jesus' sibling. He was the first pastor of a community still reeling from Resurrection. He led a fellowship of Jews who believed the Messiah had come, but who still lived under Roman pressure, priestly hostility, and internal tensions over Gentile inclusion. James was a bridge—between Torah and Gospel, between synagogue and ekklesia, between Israel's story and the nations' awakening.

James did not bear that weight alone. Early Jewish memory also remembers Simeon/Simon Clopas—identified as a cousin of Jesus and named by Hegesippus as James' successor in Jerusalem—as another link in this family line of shepherds.[4] If James is the first pastor of the Last Days, Simeon is the second: a quiet, almost hidden figure who carries on the same work of guarding a Jewish-Christian flock under growing Roman suspicion and internal turmoil. Together they embody a pattern that runs through this whole book: the leadership of Jesus' own family, not as a dynasty of

1. Luther, "Preface to the Epistles of St. James and St. Jude," 395–398.

2. Bauckham, *Jude and the Relatives of Jesus in the Early Church*, 14–20.

3. Nanos, *Mystery of Romans*, 4, 16, 34, 73, 155, states Paul's thoroughly Jewish location, his diagnosis of gentile Christian misperceptions, and his framing of gentile believers as "righteous gentiles" within a halakhic logic "works of the Law" identity as part of empire wide *religio licit* rather than a replacement identity.

4. Bauckham, *Jude and the Relatives of Jesus*, 73–103.

power, but as a line of wounded guardians holding the community together while history shakes around them with persecution and famine.[5]

And in the decades after James and Simeon, that shaking would take a liturgical form. As the rabbis at Yavneh began to reorganize Jewish life after the destruction of the Temple, a short petition—*Birkat haMinim*, the "blessing against the sectarians"—was added to the synagogue prayers.[6] In some versions, it appears to have named the Netzarim/Notzrim alongside other groups seen as dangerous to Israel's fragile recovery.[7] To stand in a synagogue and hear that line was to feel, in real time, that the room which had once been your spiritual home was now being asked to pray you out.[8] I mention it here not to rehearse grievances, but to underline how costly James' bridge-building vocation really was. The habits he teaches—mercy, patience, guarding the tongue, refusing partiality—were not theory. They were the only way a community could survive even when the liturgy of its own people began to close the door.

To understand James, we must first understand Jerusalem. James led the first community that lived the Sermon on the Mount as its daily constitution. Their rhythms—caring for widows, supporting the poor, refusing partiality, praying at set hours—were not methods of earning salvation. They were inherited habits of a people shaped by covenant and sharpened by the trauma of exile. Faith expressed itself not merely in feeling, but in fidelity; not in abstraction, but in action; not in doctrine alone, but in the shared life of a community waiting for the Son of Man.

James' famous line—"*faith without works is dead*"—is not a polemic against Paul; it is a defense of a people under pressure (see James 2:14–26). When famine hit Judea, when persecution pushed believers into hiding, when poverty crushed the weak and wealth seduced the powerful, James' call was simple: hold onto the habits that hold us. Faith is not simply what we profess; it is what endures.

5. Josephus, *Antiquities* 20.51–53; Acts 11:27–30. See Tabor, *Jesus Dynasty*.

6. b. Berakhot 28b–29a (Steinsaltz); t. Berakhot 3:25. See also Langer, *Cursing the Christians?*

7. Ehrlich and Langer, "Earliest Texts of the Birkat Haminim," 63–112 (esp. the Genizah/rite variants that include "Notzrim"). See Brown, *Birth of the Messiah*, 46, the Nazarene or Netzarim.

8. Kimelman, "Birkat Ha-Minim and the Lack of Evidence," 226–244, 391–403; Langer, *Cursing the Christians*, 17, 28–30, 38–39. As a historian of Jewish liturgy—she treats it as a prayer text with a long transmission history, not as a simple "anti-Christian slogan" that can be read straight back into the first century.

James understood that eschatology is never neutral. It either steadies us or distorts us. In Jerusalem, apocalyptic expectation was thick in the air. Some groups withdrew into caves. Others armed themselves for revolt. Others drowned themselves in mystical speculation. James resisted all of it. He steered his community into a different future—not one defined by panic or politics, but by perseverance, humility, and mercy.

James does not lead like an empire-builder or a roaming visionary. He leads like the head of a household. His authority is not centrifugal but centripetal—holding people together. This is qahal leadership: guarding fidelity so witness does not outrun character.

Acts 15 and the Repair of the Path

The heart of his leadership appears most clearly in Acts 15—the Jerusalem Council. Here was the crisis of the first generation: How do Gentiles enter the people of God? Must they live as Jews? Must they be circumcised? Must they take on Israel's full covenantal obligations?

The debate was intense. Some insisted that fidelity required full conversion. Others feared that the influx of Gentiles would dilute Jewish identity. Paul and Barnabas testified about signs and wonders among the nations. Peter recalled his encounter with Cornelius. And into the tension, James stood, listened, and then spoke with clarity that still shapes the Church today: "We should not trouble the Gentiles who turn to God" (Acts 15:19).

James did not lower the bar; he repaired the path. In the Council of Jerusalem (Acts 15), he discerned a way for the nations to worship Israel's God without becoming Jews—by requiring a basic covenantal floor that preserves table-fellowship and renounces idolatry and blood. He was not inventing a new system so much as retrieving an older logic already present in Scripture and later articulated in Jewish tradition as the obligations of the "sons of Noah." Augustine reads the apostolic decree in exactly this direction, linking the Gentile requirements to Noah and even to the "ark" as a figure of the one people of God—Jews and Gentiles held together in a shared covenantal life.[9]

9. Augustine, *Contra Faustum* 32.13 (on Acts 15 and the "ark of Noah" as a figure for Jew–Gentile unity, with discussion of abstaining from blood); cf. Gen 9:4–6; Acts 15:20, 29. For later rabbinic articulation of the "sons of Noah" framework (sheva mitzvot b'nei Noach), see b. Sanhedrin 56a–57a; t. Avodah Zarah 9:4. (Steinsaltz).

Acts 15 is the beating heart of James' ministry. It is not a bureaucratic meeting; it is a covenantal moment. Here, the Early Church chooses mercy over coercion, clarity over control, and unity over uniformity. James, the brother of Jesus, stands not as a gatekeeper and not of a new religion but as a shepherd.[10]

When I first studied this passage deeply—in Rome, far from where I grew up—I realized how contemporary it is. Italy became a living classroom for me. In that mix of Catholic friends, Muslim refugees, secular neighbors, and Jewish teachers online, I experienced firsthand how easily we project our anxieties onto other people's faith. We guard borders God never drew. We erect hurdles God never requested. But James shows us that the Gospel is not protected by walls. It is protected by wisdom. The wisdom from above—James says—is pure, peaceable, open to reason, full of mercy. This is the only wisdom strong enough for the Last Days.

The Tongue and the Test of Mercy

James' pastoral heart appears again in his emphasis on speech. "*The tongue is a fire*," he warns. Words can either build a fellowship or burn it down. Coming from a family where misunderstandings lasted years—where absence could wound as deeply as presence could heal—I know the truth of this. My brother's death reopened old silences in me, "blame games": things unsaid, things undone. James would understand. He knew the weight of family. He knew what it meant to lead while grieving. He knew how fragile a community becomes when fear governs speech.[11]

This is why James speaks so strongly about partiality, favoritism, and division. He refuses to let wealth dictate honor or poverty dictate worth. In a city like Jerusalem, where class, ethnicity, and politics collided daily, James insisted that the *ekklesia* mirror God's character: the lowly lifted, the stranger welcomed, the poor defended, the orphan protected. In James, eschatology becomes ethics. The nearness of the coming Lord becomes fuel for compassion, not reaction.[12]

James does not appear as a lone monarch, and the Twelve do not appear as free agents. Jerusalem functions as a center of gravity: a community with elders, a living memory of Jesus, and a responsibility to guard covenant

10. Fredriksen, *When Christians Were Jews*, 136–53.

11. Johnson, *Letter of James*, 244–70.

12. Moo, *Letter of James*, 168–77.

fidelity. The Twelve, meanwhile, embody Jesus' public commissioning—witnesses who preach, suffer, and plant communities. When the movement is faithful, the Twelve do not compete with the family; they remain tethered to Jerusalem's discernment even as their mission ranges outward.

Torat Edom and the Habits That Hold

And this returns us to the broader theme—Torat Edom, the wound and the healing, the way Esau and Jacob, Jew and Gentile, are brought into a single story of mercy. James embodies that healing instinct. He is the descendant of Jacob who welcomes the children of Esau. He is the Jewish elder who affirms the Gentile believer. He is the shepherd who refuses to let fear define the future.

Maybe Mary, James, and Jude understood this from the start: "last days" isn't the end of the world. It's the end of amnesia—God's people remembering who they are and living accordingly until the city finally comes down. "*Strengthen your hearts*," he writes, "*for the coming of the Lord is at hand*" (James 5:8). Not panic. Not frenzy. Strength. Steadiness. Fidelity, for in the end, life is short.

James wisely teaches us the habits that hold a community together when everything else starts to shake—how to listen before we speak, how to show mercy without performing it, how to stay humble, how to be patient, how to honor the poor, how to guard the tongue. He teaches us how to pray with others, not just alone. He teaches us how to trust God when the world convulses. That's why James stands as a pastor for the Last Days—not because he gives us a chart, but because he forms a people who can endure.

- Mary gives us the song.
- James gives us the way of life.
- Together, they prepare us to hear Jesus.

And in an age of agitation and suspicion, James' voice still cuts through with a line that feels almost too simple to be true: "*Let patience have its perfect work*" (James 1:4). There's nothing flashy about his counsel. His work isn't dramatic. His rhythm isn't sensational. His wisdom doesn't shout. Yet in the Kingdom of God, the quietest voices often carry the deepest truth.

James shows us that the Last Days do not need more speculation. They need more faithfulness—communities that can endure, families that can heal, churches that can hold together, hearts that can stay merciful when fear is trying to make them cruel. This is the gift of James—Jesus' brother, Jerusalem's shepherd, Israel's son, and the Church's first pastor for the Last Days.

Chapter 5—**Jude: The Mercy That Contends**

"Keep yourselves in the love of God, waiting for the mercy of our Lord Jesus Christ that leads to eternal life."

—Jude 21

"These are spots in your feasts of charity, when they feast with you, feeding themselves without fear: clouds they are without water, carried about of winds; trees whose fruit withereth, without fruit, twice dead, plucked up by the roots; raging waves of the sea, foaming out their own shame; wandering stars, to whom is reserved the blackness of darkness for ever."

—Jude 1:12–13 (KJV)

"To those who are called, beloved in God the Father and kept for Jesus Christ."

—Jude 1:1

If Mary gives us the tone of Christian hope and James gives us the texture of Christian faithfulness, Jude gives us the courage required to keep faith alive when everything begins to shake. He writes not as a distant theologian, but as one who knew Jesus as Lord and brother—and who watched the early movement strain under pressures both external and internal. Modern scholarship is still catching up to Jude's complexity;

Richard Bauckham notes that it remains one of the New Testament's most misunderstood texts.[1]

Jude has often been read as severe, but the shape of his letter tells another story. It is framed by mercy. He opens with a blessing: "*May mercy, peace, and love be multiplied to you*" (Jude 1:2). He ends with the assurance that God can keep you from stumbling. Jude warns the church—both the outward-going witness and the gathered assembly—because he loves it. He contends because he remembers.[2]

By Jude's lifetime, the story of Esau and Jacob had taken on a new, bitterly ironic form. The Edomites, once living on Israel's border, had been forcibly absorbed into Judea under the Hasmoneans. From that coerced fusion emerged the Herodian dynasty—Idumean in origin yet propped up by Rome as "King of the Jews." In other words, Edom was now sitting on David's throne by imperial appointment. In that world, talk of rival claimants, distorted memory, and false "anointed ones" was not abstract. It was daily life.[3]

A World Losing Its Memory

Jude lived during the unraveling of the first generation. The Temple was on the verge of destruction. The Jesus movement was splintering. Roman violence, sectarian agendas, esoteric speculation, and internal fatigue all threatened the fragile Jewish-Christian community. Jude saw what many missed: movements rarely collapse from persecution alone; more often, they collapse from forgetting who they are.

This is why Jude calls the community to contend. Not fight—contend: to hold fast under pressure, to stay grounded when the ground itself is moving, to preserve what was delivered rather than reinvent it. Jude is not defending an institution. He is defending a family story.

Jude's worldview is deeply Jewish. When he references Enoch or the angels who "*did not keep their own domain*," he is not inviting us into mythology, but reminding us that spiritual and moral rebellion always travel together (Jude 1:6, NASB). Whenever truth is distorted, relationships

1. Bauckham, *Jude and the Relatives of Jesus in the Early Church*, 157.

2. Green, *Jude* and *2 Peter*, 57–62.

3. Fredriksen, *When Christians Were Jews*, chs. 6–7; see Josephus, *Antiquities* 13.257–258 (Hasmonean incorporation of Idumea) and 14.385 (Herod's appointment in Roman context).

fray; whenever pride rises, mercy collapses.[4] Jude knows theology only works when character holds.

The Antichrist and the Wandering Stars

Jude faced more than moral drift; he faced a battle over memory. The first generations after Jesus were not only around during a time of persecution or doctrinal dispute—it a time when the story itself was contested. Names, relationships, and key events were remembered, reshuffled, and reassigned by those looking back.

Most readers have never heard of the early Jewish counter-memories preserved in the Teliya/Ma'aseh Talui or "hanged man" traditions.[5] Yet these fragments combined with portions discussed in the Talmud—far older than the medieval habit of quoting a "Jesus in the Talmud" boiling in excrement—open a window into the first century itself.[6] They preserve scrambled echoes of the Jesus movement and echoes that are not about Jesus of Nazareth at all but about a distorted Yeshu Notzri figure who inherits his name and story in polemical form through later conflations.[7]

In these "hanged man" traditions, some claim Joses (Joseh), one of Jesus' brothers, has a son with Maria Magdelene from an illegitimate relationship. Jesus' brother is named alongside Jude in the Gospel lists—begins to surface in later retellings in ways that sometimes collapse identities, drawing Mary Magdalene and other family figures into overlapping roles. Some reconstructions suggest that the woman caught in adultery (see John 8) may preserve an echo of Jesus stepping in to protect his brother Joses and a woman—possibly Mary Magdalene—caught in a public scandal.

But we should be careful: John 7:53–8:11 has a complicated manuscript history and seems to have circulated as a floating unit, appearing in different locations before it settled into John's Gospel.[8] That kind of

4. Charlesworth, *Old Testament Pseudepigrapha*, Vol. 1, for accessible primary-text context to Jude's Second Temple background register in terms of the Enochian Corpus.

5. For Ma'aseh Talui textual study see Wiki Noah in Recommended Reading and Bibliography.

6. b. Gittin 56b–57a, (Steinsaltz).

7. Schäfer, *Jesus in the Talmud*; Goldstein, "Traditions Concerning the Origin of the Toledot Yeshu," 147–82; see Wagenseil, *Tela Ignea Satanae* as an early modern example of polemical Christian publishing that amplified weaponized reception.

8. Knust and Wasserman, "Pericope of the Adulteress (John 7:53–8:11)," 22–55.

mobility creates precisely the conditions in which later communities can reframe an episode, reattach it to contested names, and utilize it as evidence or weaponize it for boundary-making. So, the proposal is plausible—not as a settled conclusion, but as a disciplined hypothesis within a world where memory, identity, and polemic were constantly tugging at the story's seams.[9]

Out of the broader Teliya narrative, a child of such a union emerges in later memory under the name "Ben Stada"—remembered in some strands of tradition as a failed insurrectionary or Egyptian-style magician—who is then stoned, hung on a carob tree, and buried at Lod.[10] Whatever one makes of the tradition-history, the New Testament shows that the apostolic movement already possessed a grammar for this kind of deception.

It warns repeatedly against *religion as power*—signs that mimic heaven while bending people away from covenant fidelity. That is why Jude reaches for the old names: Balaam (profit-driven spiritual seduction) and Korah (rebellion against lawful order) (see Jude 11), and why Peter echoes the same warning (see 2 Pet. 2:15). Paul, too, can speak of the clash as spiritual and moral—not merely intellectual—when he contrasts Christ with Belial (see 2 Cor. 6:15). The point is not that every later polemical memory is confirmed by the NT, but that the apostles already recognized the pattern: charismatic counterfeit, lawless leverage, and a community pulled off its true course.

In older Jewish imagination, the Teliya is not only the wood of hanging but also a kind of fixed point language—an axis by which order is perceived and guarded. *Sefer Yetzirah* crystallizes this register with its line: "Teli is in the World like a king on his throne; the Wheel is in the Year like a king in the city; the Heart is in the Person like a king in war." And this is precisely where medieval Rabbi Abraham Abulafia helps: not as a first-century witness, but as a Jewish reader of *Sefer Yetzirah's* received cosmology who shows how "Teli" language can function as a theological grammar of order, governance, and true orientation rather than mere astronomy.[11] Scripture itself uses the heavens as a grammar of ordered governance: the lights are set "for signs and seasons" and to "rule" the day and night, and Job can

9. Knust and Wasserman, *To Cast the First Stone*, 9–10, 46, 54.

10. Schäfer, *Jesus in the Talmud*; b. Sanhedrin 67a; b. Shabbat 104b (Steinsaltz).

11. Sefer Yetzirah 6:2; Abraham Abulafia, Gan Naul (1289).

speak of God binding constellations and establishing the "ordinances of the heavens" —a cosmic order that stands in judgment.[12]

That helps clarify why Jude's language about "wandering stars" (see Jude 13) is so sharp: stars that refuse their appointed course—unmoored lights, drifting off and dragging others with them.[13] Richard Bauckham notes that Jude's image is not random poetic insult but draws on a familiar Second Temple pattern in 1 Enoch 80:6: the "stars" that go astray from their appointed paths, an apocalyptic way of speaking about disorder, rebellion, and the seductive power of false guides.[14]

In Jude, the point is pastoral and urgent: these teachers do not merely hold wrong ideas; they function like disoriented lights—promising direction while quietly training the community to drift. And it stands in quiet contrast to the promise of the Morning Star in the letter to Thyatira—a daughter-assembly that must resist false teaching and hold fast until the dawn (see Rev. 2:24–28). Jude's "wandering stars" are counterfeit lights; the Morning Star is a gift of the true King. One kind of star pulls you off course; the other anchors you to the coming day.[15]

In the interlude on "*Behold your Mother*" and the Jerusalem above, we saw the faithful woman and the true mother-city; here Jude exposes what happens when rival stories try to unhook that mother from her true star. Seen this way, Jude's "wandering stars" belong to the same discernment-world later dramatized in the *Acts of Peter*: rival claimants and "signs" that mimic heaven, but only to pull the community off its true course.[16]

The story is populated with characters who embody competing kinds of authority. Peter appears not as a polished institution-builder but as a traveling witness—steady, prayerful, and unglamorous—whose power is bound to confession, endurance, and the name of Jesus rather than to spectacle. Opposite him stands Simon Magus, the archetype of the dazzling rival: a figure who trades in power, stagecraft, and public amazement, whose signs are designed to win attention and control a crowd. Around

12. Stars as fixed order / appointed courses (creation order as covenant stability): Gen. 1:14–18; Ps. 19:1–6; Ps. 136:7–9; Ps. 147:4; Isa. 40:26; Job 38:31–33; Jer. 31:35–36; Jer. 33:20–26.

13. Stars as true/false guidance (faithful "morning star" vs. wandering/falling lights): Num. 24:17; Matt. 2:1–10; Isa. 14:12; Dan. 8:10; Jude 13; Rev. 2:26–28; Rev. 8:10–11; Rev. 9:1; Rev. 12:4.

14. Bauckham, *Jude, 2 Peter*, 88–89.

15. Jude 1:12–13; Rev. 2:24–28; Rev. 22:16.

16. Eusebius, *Ecclesiastical History* Acts of Peter (*Actus Petri cum Simone*),

them gather vulnerable households and impressionable communities—people who want healing, certainty, and direction and who can be pulled by whatever light burns brightest in the moment. The drama turns on a simple question: what kind of wonder leads to worship, and what kind of wonder merely recruits?

What makes the *Acts of Peter* resonate with Jude is not that it is a second canon, but that it dramatizes a perennial pastoral crisis: the Church must learn to distinguish between signs that serve truth and signs that replace it. In the narrative, the most dangerous teacher is not the one who denies God outright, but the one who mimics heaven—borrowing religious language, offering counterfeit deliverance, and turning spiritual hunger into dependency. Jude calls such leaders "wandering stars" because they promise orientation while drifting from the appointed course; the *Acts of Peter* gives those stars a face—charismatic, persuasive, and intoxicating—so the Church can feel the stakes. The point is the same in both: rival stories do not merely argue; they re-train desire, redirect loyalty, and quietly pull a people off their true path.

The "false teacher" opposed in Jude may not be a distant outsider but a family rival—a competing claimant within the house of David. Messianic confusion does not arise in a vacuum; it arises when competing Davidic claimants and tangled family stories begin to circulate. The result is more than slander; it is evidence that the story of Jesus and His family was being actively contested.[17]

As I look at the Gospels, Joses/Joseh stands quietly in the background, appearing in burial scenes and family lists. But in these early Jewish narratives, Joses is recast as an alternate or even apostate figure, drafted into a rival storyline that pushes back against the growing Netzar/Notzri community. Mary Magdalene, likewise, becomes entangled in these counter-narratives, her role stretched and distorted in ways that may help explain how later imaginations—right down to modern "Jesus and Mary as a couple" theories—found their raw material.

Here, even James D. Tabor, who makes no reference to the Teliya, provides insight. In *The Jesus Dynasty,* he argues as mentioned with James and Simon Clopas, the original Jesus movement was dynastic in character:

17. Boyarin, *Jewish Gospels*, ch. 5, useful for locating "high" categories within Jewish interpretive worlds; employed here for conceptual framing rather than as a direct source for the Teliya claims. His value in this paragraph is to keep the reader from assuming that "messianic rivalry" and "elevated claimant language" must be late, foreign, or purely "Christian" inventions.

Jesus as royal Davidic Messiah, with his brothers (James, Simon, Jude, Joses) and other relatives—the Desposyni—forming a continuing leadership line after His death. He also notes the now-famous tombstone of Tiberius Julius Abdes Pantera, a Sidonian archer in the Roman army buried in what is now Germany, whose name has been drawn into discussions of the later Pandera traditions.

In terms of ancient symbolism, "panther" and "lion" belong to the same family of royal big-cat imagery, which resonates uncomfortably with the "Lion of Judah" messianic title and helps explain why a name like Pantera could so readily be pulled into messianic and anti-messianic storytelling. Tabor treats the connection with proper caution, but his work still confirms the broader picture: a first-century world in which Jesus' family line, Davidic legitimacy, and questions of paternity and succession were live, contested issues.[18]

Even the infamous "number of the beast" (666) was the kind of riddle ancient audiences could decode through letter–number equivalences (gematria/isopsephy). Many interpreters argue it most plausibly encodes Nero Caesar when the name is transliterated into Hebrew characters (nrwn qsr = 50 + 200 + 6 + 50 + 100 + 60 + 200 = 666)—an instance of numerology used in the war of allegiance and identity.[19] But the same technique can be re-deployed polemically in later memory: if one writes "Yeshu Notzri" in a defective Hebrew spelling (ישו נצרי), its standard values also total 666 (ישו = 316; נצרי = 350) all with the seven heads and ten crowns part of the Hebrew letters.[20]

The point is not that gematria proves theology, but that symbolic numbering can become a weapon: what first functioned as coded critique can later be turned into coded slander. And whatever later polemics do with numbers, the New Testament's own diagnosis is starker: the "spirit of antichrist" is not merely a future calendar problem but a present distortion already "in the world" (see 1 John 4:3), leaving residual effects in communities long after the first conflict has passed.

So, later communities could weaponize the number itself as an identity slur inside boundary disputes. That later polemical move should not be treated as a historical identification of Jesus of Nazareth in the Gospels; it functions as numerological rhetoric within a contested "Yeshu/Notzri/

18. Tabor, *Jesus Dynasty*, 64–72.

19. Koester, "Revelation Numbers"; Koester, *Revelation*.

20. WikiNoah, https://www.wikinoah.org/en/index.php/Ye.Sh.U._NoTzRY

Netzer" memory-stream rather than a sober referent in Revelation's first-century setting. Later polemical tradition also developed acronymic readings around "Yeshu," treating the name as a hostile backronym (e.g., "may his name/memory be blotted out"); whatever one concludes historically, it shows how naming itself became a boundary marker in later conflicts.[21]

If some of these terms are unfamiliar, don't get stuck on the labels. What matters is the reality: rival stories about Jesus and his family started early, and Jude is fighting to keep the received Gospel from being rewritten—by people who had heard of Jesus but didn't truly know Him.

None of this should surprise us. Jesus Himself warned that "many will come in my name" and deceive many—false messiahs and false prophets who would lead people astray (see Matt. 24; Mark 13; Luke 21). Those warnings are often projected into a distant future, but Jude reads like a letter written from inside the first wave of their outworking. He is not shadowboxing a hypothetical Antichrist centuries later; he is answering concrete deceivers in his own world—teachers and rival voices close enough to pass as insiders, perhaps even close enough to brush the edges of his wider kin-network.

That proximity is exactly what makes the danger acute: counterfeit memory is most persuasive when it speaks with familiar accents. And it helps explain why later Christian and Jewish polemical traditions—texts like the *Acts of Peter* and (in a very different register) contested materials associated with the Teliya—can feel like they are breathing the same air: rival claimants, competing signs, and stories that mimic holiness in order to pull a community off its true course. This is not a Da Vinci Code-style detour into secret documents and thriller revelations, nor an invitation to let later "gnostic Gospels" dictate the plot. It is simply the sober New Testament claim that the struggle over Jesus' name began early, close to home, and that Jude is one of the first guardians who names it plainly.[22]

These early conflations are not random. They reflect a world in which:

- many had heard about Jesus,
- fewer truly knew Him,

21. Schäfer, *Jesus in the Talmud*, 129–45.

22. Matt. 24:4–5, 11, 23–26; Mark 13:5–6, 21–23; Luke 21:8; Jude 3–4, 12–13, 17–19; 1 John 2:18–23; 2 Thess. 2:1–12. For a later dramatization of rival "signs" and contested apostolic authority. For the broader phenomenon of "gnostic gospels" as later alternative retellings rather than first-generation apostolic testimony, see the standard discussions in the introductions to critical editions/collections of Nag Hammadi materials.

- and only His family and faithful witnesses guarded the Evangelion as they had received it.

Jude writes into that world—not only to call his readers back from moral collapse, but to steady the memory of Jesus against rival claimants and counter-narratives that threatened to rewrite the story from inside the house of David itself.

Again, to reiterate, this chapter distinguishes sharply between earlier Teliya/Teliyat Yeshu strata (which he treats as a fragile Jewish counter-memory standing in the shadow of the Passion and reflecting real intra-Jewish conflict) and the much later Toledot Yeshu literature. Whatever one concludes about the earliest layers and their transmission, the *Toledot Yeshu* that survives in manuscript form is widely treated in scholarship as a medieval (with much editing) satirical counter-history—a polemical "anti-Gospel" that inverts New Testament motifs and relocates the Jesus story into a framework designed to mock and refute Christian claims rather than preserve historical memory.

At the same time, the phrase *Toledot Yeshu* can also function more innocently as a straightforward Hebrew rendering of Matthew 1:1 ("book/account of the genealogy of Jesus"). In fact, Hebrew Matthew materials and modern Hebrew renderings can open with wording like ("Sefer Toledot Yeshua ha-Mashiach . . . "). This overlap likely encouraged later conflation in popular reception. But the deeper point is how words themselves perpetuate conflations: Jude slides toward Judas, Yeshu toward Jesus, and the resulting narrative becomes a weapon rather than a witness.

Once Christian polemicists began circulating versions of the *Toledot* as "proof" of Jewish blasphemy, the text could be pulled into a wider ecosystem of accusation and coercion—an evil campaign that included state-backed campaigns against Jewish books (most notoriously, the thirteenth-century prosecutions and public burnings of the *Talmud*).[23] The *Toledot Yeshu*, in other words, is not the Jewish memory being retrieved here; it is a later deformation that proved easy to weaponize—both against Jews and, indirectly, against the possibility of careful historical distinctions within Jewish and Hebrew Gospel contexts.

23. Meerson and Schäfer's Princeton project (2014) is explicitly framed as a philological/database enterprise—collecting and transcribing manuscripts to enable comparison of *Toledot Yeshu* "macro- and microforms" and tracking development across versions—rather than an attempt to read the material from within a rabbinic self-understanding (e.g., as guarded oral tradition or as a lineage-claim about "what the rabbis meant").

These texts have left many Jewish communities with an aversion to the name, closed and hardened. If Jude is fighting "intruders" and "wandering stars," then part of the fight is not only ethics but identity—who counts as the true witness, whose story gets told, and which claimant gets remembered. The later *Ma'aseh Talui*/Nittel ecosystem shows how, downstream, Jewish and Christian worlds kept re-hanging the story on different hooks—until rival biographies formed around the same haunted names.[24]

Guarding the Real Story

Jude's task, then, was not only theological but historical. He was preserving the real story in a world where false Jesuses—just as Jesus Himself had warned—were already beginning to appear. Alternative genealogies and counterfeit revelations were already circulating. Some versions elevated a false messiah; others denigrated the true family; still others aligned Jesus with Roman power or anti-covenantal movements. In this context, Jude's plea to "contend for the faith" becomes sharper, clearer, more human:

- If the memory is lost, the message is lost.
- If the story fractures, the community fractures.

Jude writes as a guardian of the family's testimony, standing in continuity with the line of relatives who carried this burden before and after him. That burden included guarding the Name (HaShem) itself in a world where even healings could become battlegrounds—something preserved, in a hostile register, in the ben Dama tradition about healing "in the name of Yeshu."[25] In other words, the controversy was never only about whether a cure "worked," but about what kind of authority—and what kind of messianic claim—was being smuggled in under the cover of healing.

Beside James the Just in Jerusalem and Simeon/Simon Clopas—remembered in early sources as a cousin of Jesus and James' successor in the

24. Nittel/Nittel Nacht (lit. "Nativity Night," often explained as deriving from Latin *Natale*/*Natalis*) refers to an Ashkenazi folk custom—attested especially in parts of medieval and early-modern Christian Europe—associated with Christmas Eve (and in some places also Jan. 6).

25. t. Ḥullin 2:22–24; b. Avodah Zarah 16b–17a (Steinsaltz) Eleazar ben Dama healing-in-the-name tradition as a boundary-marker unit.

city,[26] Jude may well be the last living voice able to say, in effect: This is who He truly is. This is the story as we lived it.

Mercy as Warfare

This contested landscape makes Jude's emphasis on mercy even more astonishing. "*Have mercy on those who doubt.*" (Jude 22) These words come from a man who had every reason to become defensive, territorial, or combative. But Jude remembers what it meant for his own family to misunderstand Jesus. He remembers his own resistance, his own disbelief (see John 7:5). He writes as a man who was shown mercy and now extends it.

For Jude, mercy is not softness; it is spiritual combat. It is how one pushes back against distortion, fear, arrogance, and despair.

- Mercy restores the community's humanity.
- Mercy protects those destabilized by false teaching.
- Mercy steadies the hearts of those shaken by crisis.

Guarding the Original Evangelion

As rabbinic leadership helped reorganize Jewish communal life in the decades after AD 70—with Yavneh (often "Jamnia" in older scholarship) emerging as a key post-Temple center—and as Gentile-Christian communities increasingly drifted from their Jewish roots, Jude reads like an early alarm against a story that could be co-opted, diluted, or bent into something else—perhaps even anticipating later boundary-marking moves associated with the Birkat ha-Minim, (the blessing on the sectarians) though the prayer's earliest form and targets remain debated.[27]

In that same widening gap, "official" Christian histories eventually get narrated through later lenses, while modern scholarship tries to reconstruct earlier layers and streams—whether through hypothetical sources like "Q" (used to explain Matthew-Luke material not in Mark) or early church manuals like *The Didache*, which preserve a snapshot of developing practice. Jewish memory, meanwhile, did not entirely lose contact with the Jesus story: we still see scattered traces of engagement with Evangelion

26. Bauckham, *Jude and the Relatives of Jesus*, 79–94.

27. Kimelman, "Birkat Ha-Minim and the Lack of Evidence," 226–244, 391–403.

traditions and later Jewish encounters with New Testament texts across diverse manuscript and polemical lines including Islam.

Jude saw movements that traded covenant fidelity for political access or replaced the Jewish Jesus with a philosophical symbol that shows up in a kind of Gnosticism whose very name sounds uncomfortably close to Notzrim.[28] The Teliya traditions preserve echoes of these anxieties.

Whether one calls these sources *Teliyat Yeshu Notzri, Ma'aseh Talui, the Strasbourg* traditions, or the early Notzri counter-narratives, they reveal a world where identity was contested and the Name (HaShem) was vulnerable to misuse. Jude enters this world not with panic, but with clarity.

- He warns.
- He intercedes.
- He points the community back to the love that first called them.

His final charge—"*Keep yourselves in the love of God*" (Jude 21) —is not a burden but a lifeline. Remain where the mercy of God already surrounds you. Trust the One who can keep you from falling.

The Family That Forms the Faith

In our age of suspicion and fragmentation, Jude's voice is exactly what we need. Mary gives us hope. James gives us habits. Jude gives us perseverance.

He does not tell us to escape the world, but to endure it. He does not tell us to win arguments, but to keep mercy alive. He does not anchor our faith in speculation, but in the God who keeps His people.

Jude stands as the last voice of Jesus' family, the guardian of the Evangelion, the shepherd who remembers the real story, the brother who learned mercy the hard way, and the elder who knew that God finishes the story He begins.

His final words are not just benediction; they are resistance:

"*To him who is able . . .*" (Jude 24)

Able to steady us.

Able to keep us.

Able to bring us home.

28. Flusser, *Jewish Sources in Early Christianity*, 55–63.

In the end, Jude teaches that mercy is how we contend, and that love—not fear—is the true power at the center of the Last Days. Jude does not write into a vacuum. The communities he guards already have a name in Jewish memory: they are the Netzarim/Notzrim—the branch-people, the watchmen on Ephraim's hills who believe the Netzer of Isaiah has appeared. They are the opposite of "wandering stars": not drifters cut loose from their hook in the heavens, but watchmen who stay at their post, guarding the covenantal story of Jesus and His family.

In chapter 8, we will follow those names—Netzarim/Notzrim—through Scripture, Jewish tradition, and history to see how a word that once meant *faithful watchman* became, in many ears, a byword for *danger*, and how recovering its first meaning may help heal some of the very wounds Jude saw opening in his own day.

Interlude 2—Graffiti on the Walls of Empire

I have never been to Jerusalem.

Nor the Rock & Roll Hall of Fame in my hometown.

But I have been to the Cross of Calvary and keep going back.

Missionaries, pastors, pilgrims, prophecy teachers—everyone seemed to make their way to the State of Israel sooner or later. They came back with stories: standing on the Mount of Olives, tracing the Via Dolorosa, touching the stones of the Western Wall—almost like brushing the hem of sacred memory.

I never did.

However . . .

In 2022, flying to an Alliance regional meeting in the Hashemite Kingdom of Jordan, I finally stood in the land where Jesus once walked—on the Decapolis side of the Jordan River—looking west across the hills a little like Moses, only with an iPhone in my hand and Pink Floyd in my ears. I found myself looking over the Jordan with "Sheep" (from *Animals*) playing, and the old line of Scripture would not let me go: "*We are regarded as sheep to be slaughtered*" (see Ps. 44:22; Rom. 8:36). From that ridge, I could see the State of Israel, breathe the same dry air, and feel the tension in my bones: one foot in the Roman world of the Gospels, one eye on a modern political reality that now bears an ancient name—and what a mess.

And it forced an admission. For me, the modern "Holy Land trip" often felt like backward-facing tourism—reenactment without revelation. Yes, you can glean real insight; the geography does teach. But my aversion to political Zionism (not the spiritual Zion of A. B. Simpson) made the whole enterprise feel less like pilgrimage and more like participation in a story that too easily baptizes injustice—toward Jews and toward Arabs—by treating Israel as a political fulfilled guarantee rather than a covenantal summons.

Ironically, the closest I have ever stood to the apocalyptic Jesus was not in Jerusalem at all, but in Rome—the city that destroyed the Temple, reshaped Jewish memory for two millennia, and later claimed to sit on the chair of Peter.

Even here in Orlando—where we have just returned for home assignment (sometimes called furlough)—the theme-park "Holy Land Experience" no longer exists. I remember taking my daughter there 25 years ago when it first opened and stirred controversy. The imitation Jerusalem is gone. The real one remains a place I have still only seen from across the Jordan.

- Rome is where I learned to see Jesus again.
- Not the sentimental Jesus of devotional art.
- Not the imperial Jesus of triumphal architecture.

But the Jewish Jesus whose world was torn apart by the empire whose ruins I walked among daily—and the Jesus whom the Church, in her own way, adorned, tamed, and sometimes obscured.

Our church met on the edge of the Roman Forum. I studied at the Angelicum and ate lunch at the Gregorian. I worshiped beside believers from Asia, Africa, South America, and the Middle East. I listened to refugees, diplomats, secular seekers, and priests. And somehow, Rome made Jerusalem clearer.

Whenever visitors wanted my "religiously incorrect tour," I knew exactly where to take them. We'd start at "Piazza Martino Lutero" (yes there really is one) and then walk toward the Colosseum—but not through the gate where the story is packaged and sold. I'd bring them down a narrow road to the one free vantage point where you can glimpse the inside of the Arch of Titus without buying a ticket.

The Arch was raised with the spoils of the Temple's destruction. It doesn't just commemorate a victory; it petrifies a wound. On its inner wall, Roman soldiers carry off the menorah as if covenant light could be seized and paraded.[1] And the Colosseum—empire's theater of power—was built in the afterglow of Jerusalem's plunder.[2]

Standing there, I always felt the weight of the Gospels in a way no pilgrimage brochure ever offered me.

- The Arch does not lie.
- It exposes the catastrophe Jesus wept over.
- It reveals the world His earliest followers had to navigate.
- It shows why His warnings were not metaphor, but mercy.

In the shadow of Caesar's boast, I finally understood why Jesus cried, "How often I have longed to gather your children . . ." (Matt. 23:37, NIV).

- It is one thing to read those words.
- It is another to stand before the empire that crushed the city He loved.
- Some people discover Jesus in Jerusalem.

I discovered Him by not going.

The Donkey Among Caesars (and the Real Peter)

Not far from the Arch of Titus—high on the Palatine Hill where the Caesars lived—there is another testimony. Smaller. Rougher. In its own way, more honest than any basilica. In the quarters where household servants once lived, archaeologists uncovered a crude etching on plaster: the *Alexamenos graffito*. At first glance it looks almost childish. A man stands with his hand raised in worship before a crucified figure—except the crucified one has the head of a donkey. Underneath, in shaky Greek, someone scratched: "Alexamenos worships his god."[3]

It was meant as mockery. But for me, it has become one of the most profound images in Rome.

1. Arch of Titus: Temple spoils. The Arch's inner relief shows the Temple spoils carried in triumph, including the menorah.

2. Colosseum and Judaean spoils. Multiple modern summaries report that construction was funded from booty/"general's share of the spoil" after the Jewish War and Jerusalem's fall (70 CE).

3. Alexamenos graffito. The graffito (Palatine Hill / Domus Gelotiana area) includes the Greek caption commonly rendered "*Alexamenos worships (his) god.*"

Here—on the back wall of Caesar's world—a nobody named Alexamenos is ridiculed for worshiping a crucified Jew. His God is drawn with the head of a donkey: the most ridiculous god Rome could imagine. And yet for anyone formed by Israel's Scriptures, the insult boomerangs. The donkey is the animal of humble kingship—the beast that carried Messiah into Jerusalem. And the donkey also sits inside Torah as a redemption law: the firstborn donkey (*petter chamor*) must be ransomed with a lamb (or kid), and if it is not redeemed, its neck is broken.[4]

That matters because this isn't just symbolism. Jewish families still practice *pidyon ha-ben*—the redemption of a firstborn son—by giving the redemption price to a *kohen* when the child is eligible.[5] And the donkey mitzvah remains halakhic too—rare today because few people own donkeys, but still real in the logic of Torah: "firstbornness" and "redemption" are covenant realities, not religious poetry.[6]

In Jewish teaching, the donkey can become a parable of the nations: stubborn, unclean, unable to bear holiness on their own—yet spared through the lamb that stands in their place. And in the West, the donkey has often been slandered as stupid or ridiculous, when in Scripture it is the creature that sees what Balaam cannot and obeys when a "seer" is blind.

Somewhere in this same city, tradition says Peter was crucified. I once attended a seminar at the Angelicum where a presenter, half-joking, said they had Peter's bones "in a cigar box." Maybe there were many "Peters"—many bones, many memories, many claimants sent out in his name. But the Peter that matters for my story is the fisherman from Galilee: the man who rebuked Jesus, denied Him, and was restored.

And that restoration matters because it gives us a truer "rock" than marble ever could. If the Gospel can redeem Peter, it can redeem anybody. In Rome, I lived with two rival "Peters" in front of me:

1. The Peter of St. Peter's—ringed by *Tu es Petrus* in gold letters, enthroned above the nations.

4. Firstborn donkey law in Torah. Exod. 13:13; cf. Exod. 34:20 (redeem with a lamb/kid; otherwise break its neck).

5. Pidyon ha-ben is practiced and codified. Rooted in Num. 18:15–16 and treated as halakhah (e.g., Shulchan Arukh, Yoreh De'ah 305; widely summarized in contemporary halakhic guides).

6. Pidyon petter chamor is halakhah discussed in rabbinic sources (Tractate Bekhorot) and codified in Shulchan Arukh, Yoreh De'ah 321; modern summaries note its rarity because few Jews own donkeys.

2. The Peter suggested by that scratched wall on the Palatine—a humiliated follower of a humiliated Messiah, mocked as foolish, yet faithful to the end.

My Jewish teacher, Yossi, leans into this when he calls himself the *Pettur Chamor*—the firstborn donkey and speaks on the *Messianic Lamb Network*. He's picking up the same line: the redeemed donkey who now carries the Lamb's story to the world. That image has done more to heal my view of Peter—and the meaning of "the church built on this rock"—than any treatise.

So, like I always suspected in the Catholic–Protestant tug-of-war: we're all wrong when we make the foundation into power, it must be forgiven weakness, redeemed stubbornness, humbled strength. So, when I stand in that small Palatine museum and look at the Alexamenos graffito, I don't only see Roman contempt. I see a backhanded confirmation of an older story:

- A crucified King
- The donkey of humble procession
- A disciple who keeps worshiping anyway

Rome tried to mock the faith. It accidentally carved the logic of the Gospel into plaster. Still a small medieval witness—polemical but telling—adds an echo to the graffiti. In a text called *Sefer Ḥasidim* (Hasidei Ashkenaz), a passage about giving altered names to apostates includes a striking aside that pairs "Shimon Kefa" with the phrase *petter chamor*.[7] It is not a neutral report, and it is not "proof" of biography. But it shows something important: even in Jewish polemical memory, "Kefa/Peter" remained a live figure inside Torah categories—firstbornness, redemption, and the danger of followers going astray.

And there is an older—and even stranger—echo in the rabbinic margins. A variant tradition preserved around b. Avodah Zarah 10a, Rashi, the Great Talmud Commentator (1040–1105) is *reported* to name three Jewish figures—often glossed as Yochanan, Paulus, and Pitros—and then to add the startling claim that "these three were not heretics" because their intention was "for the good of Israel."[8] The point is not to treat a medieval

7. Sefer Ḥasidim §191 citing "Shimon Kefa" and the epithet "petter chamor."

8. Rashi on b. Avodah Zarah 10a (commentary in Sefaria)—Christianity from Israel "for Israel's benefit."

gloss as courtroom evidence for first-century biography. It is, rather, to notice what the category preserves; even where Jewish memory is wary, polemical, or protective, it can still imagine Peter and Paul inside Torah concerns—acting (rightly or wrongly) in response to Israel's distress, not simply as enemies inventing a new god.

Nor does that impulse disappear in later centuries. Into the modern era, figures such as Rabbi Jacob Emden (1697–1776) could speak of Christianity's providential role for the nations without dissolving Israel's covenantal identity.[9] The same broad posture appears again in Elijah Benamozegh (1823–1900) of Livorno—an Italian rabbi who could affirm Israel's enduring election while still imagining a meaningful, vocation for Christianity in the divine economy.

Placed beside the *Sefer Ḥasidim*—which can call "Shimon Kefa" a *tzaddiq* even while noting that others "err after him," and while preserving the Ashkenazic taunt *petter cḥamor*—the pattern is revealing. The same tradition that mocks can also concede a kind of tragic complexity: a "Kefa" who remains a live figure in Jewish moral imagination, still discussed with the vocabulary of righteousness, stumbling followers, and covenantal risk. That is exactly the space my argument inhabits: not triumphalist proof-texting, but the unsettling fact that even hostile memories sometimes keep circling back to Peter as a contested inside figure—bound up with firstbornness, redemption, and the danger of a story being hijacked.

Back in 2021, when I first met Yossi, he told me he had once made aliyah to the State of Israel seeking safety from persecution—and later left Israel for similar concerns. He became the one of the most significant voices helping me recover the Jewish Jesus, "connecting the dots" between fragments left by my years in Rome and my immersion in medieval studies.

Like him, I found myself outside the land—and, in a different sense, outside the Eternal City as well: an eternal student with no terminal degree (the one I kept telling Gloria I was working on). But this book is my attempt to make the journey intelligible—to show how, from the margins, the story sometimes comes into focus with unusual clarity when we walk with His Presence and follow a leading that baffles us in the moment.

And perhaps that is fitting. Because the Jesus, Mary, James, and Jude and the New Testaments' witnesses remembered are not confined to one geography or system. He is not locked behind checkpoints, theology,

9. Falk, "Rabbi Jacob Emden's Views on Christianity and the Noachide Commandments," 105–111. See also *Jesus the Pharisee*.

reconstructed archaeology or the Vatican Archives where I had a library card. He is not found only where He walked, but wherever His people walk in His ways—especially among those who feel displaced, unseen, or far from home.

I still hope to go to Jerusalem one day. But even if I never do, I have learned that the holiest places in the world are often where:

- wounds are faced,
- stories are reconciled,
- strangers share bread,
- and the living Jesus is recognized in the breaking of it.

Rome gave me back the Jesus I needed—the Jewish Messiah who still gathers the scattered and widens the family. Perhaps that is its own kind of pilgrimage.

Chapter 6—Jesus: The Face of the Father

"No one has ever seen God; the only Son . . . has made Him known."

—John 1:18

"Philip said to him, 'Show us the Father.' . . . Jesus said, 'Whoever has seen me has seen the Father.'"

—John 14:8–9

Jesus is often discussed as an idea, a doctrine, an argument, or a platform symbol. But before He was any of those to anyone else, Jesus was a Jewish son in a Jewish family, living inside a story far older than Christendom.

Mary shaped His earliest world. James and Jude grew up beside Him—sharing chores, meals, and the weight of a people waiting for redemption. The rhythms of Galilee—Sabbaths, psalms, harvests, and synagogues where Hebrew and Aramaic were heard (and, in many places, everyday Greek as well)—were His first world.

To make Jesus real again, we must return Him to that world.[1] Jesus did not emerge in abstraction. He did not step into history as a floating philosophy. He stepped into a covenant already in motion—Israel's vocation to bear God's Name before the nations. His imagination was formed by Israel's Scriptures: Isaiah's Servant, Daniel's Son of Man, Zechariah's humble King, Micah's Shepherd-Ruler. He was not an outsider to Judaism, and He did not present Himself as the founder of a new religion. He was Israel from within—fulfilling Israel's calling from the inside.

1. Falk, *Jesus the Pharisee*, 8, 24.

This is close to the point the late Rabbi Harvey Falk pressed in *Jesus the Pharisee*: Jesus' posture aligns less with the hardline boundary-making instincts often associated with Shammai and more with the merciful, mission-minded stream associated with Hillel—the conviction that Israel's election is not a license for spiritual hoarding, but a vocation to become a blessing to the nations.[2] In that light, Jesus' conflicts are not a conflict with "Judaism as such," but with particular leadership expressions of Judaism that could become harsh, insular, or compromised in the handling of the flock.

That distinction matters because so much Christian speech collapses "the leaders" into "the Jews" and then uses the collapse as a moral alibi. But Jesus does not attack the Jews. He speaks as a Jew to Jews, like a prophet inside Israel calling Israel back to covenant fidelity. If we want to recover the scandal and the beauty of the Gospels, we must stop treating them as an argument against Judaism and start reading them as a family-and-covenant drama unfolding within Israel's sacred story—on Israel's terms, with Israel's Scriptures open on the table.

And once Jesus is restored to His family and His people, the mission of the Church looks different too. It stops being a campaign to replace Israel and becomes what Paul says it is: Gentiles grafted into Israel's olive tree—humbled, grateful, and trembling with responsibility—so that Israel might one day look at the nations and recognize her own God being loved, honored, and obeyed (see Rom. 11). Hold the thought for Interlude 3.

When we pull Jesus away from His Jewish world, He dissolves into a silhouette—recognizable but hollow. Christian history has a name for that impulse: Docetism (from *dokein*, "to seem").[3] It is the temptation to love a Christ who appears holy and powerful yet is strangely untouched by the textures of real life—family, land, Torah, poverty, meals, blood, tears, and death. Once Jesus becomes a principle instead of Israel's embodied Messiah, the Gospel becomes easier to turn into a system, a slogan, or a tool of power.

Galilee formed Him. The Temple stirred Him. The prophets fed His imagination. The poor drew out His compassion. Everything He said rose from God's promises to Israel. Everything He did revealed what those promises always intended: mercy, healing, justice, restoration, and the nearness of the Kingdom.

2. Falk, *Jesus the Pharisee*, 8, 24.

3. Kelly, *Early Christian Doctrines*, 141.

- Jesus healed because the God of Israel heals.
- Jesus forgave because the God of Israel forgives.
- Jesus welcomed outsiders because Israel was always called to gather the nations.
- He was not inventing mercy; He was embodying it.

When Jesus preached, people did not walk away saying, "What an idea." They walked away saying, "God has visited His people." His authority was not domination, charisma, or spectacle. It was the authority of one so aligned with God that His words carried the weight of the One who sent Him.

This is why early Jewish believers reached for "branch" language—Isaiah's *netzer*—to name Him as Israel's hoped-for figure and why later memory preserves "Netzarim/Notzrim" as a designation for Jewish followers of Jesus in the first centuries.[4]

But Jesus was more than the branch. Jewish tradition also preserved language for something even more intimate: the sense that God can be encountered through a Presence capable of being revealed without being diminished. In later liturgical and interpretive streams—especially those associated with medieval Ashkenazi piety—commentary appears that speaks of Yeshua (salvation) as Sar haPanim, "Prince of the Presence," in connection with Yom Kippur themes of mediation and divine justice.[5]

What such echoes are trying to guard is not "a second power," but a biblical truth: the Holy One can be encountered through His own self-disclosure—His "face" turned toward humanity—without God being divided or diminished. God draws near—He puts His Name somewhere, He makes His face shine, He sends His messenger, His glory fills the house—yet Israel is trained to resist turning any disclosed nearness into a detachable thing that competes with God.

Within early rabbinical discussion, the warning associated with Acher—*kitzutz ba-neti'ot*, "cutting the shoots"—functions like an interpretive signpost. The mistake is not to acknowledge that God mediates His Presence in the world. The mistake is to sever that mediation from the one God and treat it as an independent authority—as if the "means" of nearness

4. Pritz, *Nazarene Jewish Christianity*, 12–17.

5. Casal, "Yeshua Sar haPanim in the Machzor for Yom Kippur."

could become a rival throne. In other words: the danger is not God is near, but nearness becomes rivalry.[6]

This is where the Gospels are both scandalous and clarifying. John does not offer a second deity. He insists that the Father is made known in the Son—not as a competitor to God, but as God's own self-revelation. The Son is not a second power alongside the Holy One; He is the Father's face turned toward Israel and the nations. "*Whoever has seen me has seen the Father*" (John 14:9).

So, how does God draw near and act? What do we do with evil? What do we do with death? In early Jewish and Christian texts, angel-language often functions as a kind of sacred shorthand for nearness: the God of Israel is not distant or sealed off from His creation—He intervenes, He sends, He guards, He judges, He heals. Susan R. Garrett helps frame this point by showing how "angel talk" is regularly a way of thinking about divine Presence and action in the face of the powers, suffering, and mortality and how those themes press toward Christological claims about Jesus.[7] And in many Muslim conversion narratives, dreams and visions (often interpreted as an appearing Jesus like angel) function as prompts that lead seekers to consult a Christian, open a Bible, or begin reading the *Injil*/New Testament.[8]

Here I challenge Michael Heiser's divine-council framework: a lens becomes a problem when it turns into a master key.[9] Once that happens, ordinary covenant language starts getting re-coded into cosmic speculation. Take Jeremiah 31:6: the "watchmen" aren't heavenly watchers; they're human watchmen—heralds calling Israel to get up and go to Zion. That matters because the prophetic text is doing something concrete: summoning a people back into covenant life. When a speculative grid outranks the text, Israel's human, historical vocabulary gets swallowed by a cosmic scheme, and we end up with fascination where Scripture is aiming for repentance, hope, and obedience. We'll unpack this more in chapter 8.

More than that, the method can subtly distort the Jewish relation of the text—not because the so-called Old Testament is unimportant, and not because Hebrew is irrelevant, but because vocabulary mastery can masquerade as covenant hearing. Knowing Hebrew and being an Old

6. On Acher and *kitzutz ba-neti'ot* ("cutting the shoots/saplings"), Structure and Ideology in the Aher Narrative (b. Ḥagigah 15a–b [Steinsaltz]).

7. Garrett, *No Ordinary Angel*.

8. Martyn, "Role of Pre-Conversion Dreams and Visions in Islam," 57–66.

9. Heiser, *Unseen Realm*, and *Reversing Hermon*.

Testament scholar does not automatically place one inside Israel's interpretive posture. In my judgment, Heiser's approach can encourage readers to treat mediation as an independent explanatory system rather than as Scripture's disciplined way of speaking about the Holy One drawing near. The result can be a flattening of Israel's covenant voice into an ontology chart—interesting, even thrilling, but not always helpful for reading Jesus, Paul, or the apostolic mission with sobriety.

I also say this as someone who studied deeply in Rome with Dominican heirs of Thomas Aquinas—long known as the *Doctor Angelicus*. Aquinas is not to be caricatured, but the medieval habit of "angelic taxonomy" can easily become a template: a way of handling spiritual reality that prizes classification over covenantal discernment. My concern is not with angels as such, but with what happens when spiritual beings become the main event. The biblical aim is not fascination but faithfulness: angel-language serves the story of God's nearness and action, and it finally presses us back toward Christ, not toward a heavenly bureaucracy.

The Bible is not embarrassed by the heavenly host. It assumes a real, ordered company of God's servants—"thousands upon thousands"—who worship, obey, and are sent (see Ps. 103:20–21; Dan. 7:10; Luke 2:13–14; Heb. 1:14; Rev. 5:11). Angels are not a rival storyline but part of the stage-lighting of God's kingship: they magnify His holiness, attend His judgments, and guard His people. And precisely because the host is real, it must remain what Scripture makes it—ministering witnesses and commissioned messengers—so that our attention stays fixed on the One they adore: the LORD Himself, revealed climactically in Israel's Messiah (see Col. 2:18–19; Rev. 19:10).

Garrett's framing is a useful corrective here: angel-language often functions as sacred shorthand for God's nearness and action in a world haunted by evil and death, and its weight presses toward Christology, not toward endless spiritual taxonomy.[10] In other words, the point is not to feed curiosity about the heavenly bureaucracy, but to strengthen fidelity to the God who intervenes—who sends, guards, judges, and heals—and who has made Himself known in Israel's Messiah, the One who could have summoned "more than twelve legions of angels," yet chose the way of the cross.

Certainly R. C. Sproul pressed a compatible pastoral point as it applies to the heart of eschatology in his book *The Last Days According to Jesus*, yet not in timelines but into total trust in the character of Christ. In

10. Garrett, *No Ordinary Angel*, 5, 237.

his later years, he loved expository preaching where the simplifier in theology brought the Word to our hearts. In other words, what God is like is what Jesus is like: "It was time, Jesus said, for the disciples to understand in a life-changing way that He is the Son of God, preferably because He said it, but if not then because His miracles proved it."[11] And that clarity helps sanctify the journey back into the Jewish world of Jesus, where this truth is not a metaphysical slogan but a covenant reality—the Father made known in the Son, steadying fear and purifying hope by the person of Jesus of Nazareth, the eternal Son.

One reason modern end-times talk becomes so anxious is that we often carry an unspoken picture of God that is more philosophical than biblical—more abstract than covenantal. In parts of Jewish, Christian, and Islamic philosophical theology, especially where Aristotelian categories were absorbed, God can be described in ways that emphasize immutability and transcendence so strongly that the living textures of Scripture—promise, Presence, jealousy, compassion, judgment, healing—begin to sound like anthropomorphic concessions rather than the very shape of revelation.

Maimonides (1138–1204), the Jewish Aristotelian, is a towering figure, and Christian theology has its own parallel streams. But he is not the referee for Yeshua Sar haPanim—that language lives in other Jewish liturgical and interpretive veins, and I believe, suppressed, yet his Torah constraints allowed divine simplicity its reign.[12] I'm not demonizing "classical theism," and I'm not saying Scripture is anti-intellectual. I'm making a pastoral point: when covenant speech is treated as secondary, Jesus becomes a concept. Divine action begins to sound like a problem to solve, not a revelation to receive. And that same thinning spills into eschatology—so "last days" talk turns into metaphysical speculation or political code instead of covenant warning, covenant mercy, and covenant endurance.

Jesus brings us back to the biblical center: not an abstract deity behind the text, but the Father made known in the Son—God acting, promising, judging, forgiving, healing, and gathering. And that "gathering" has an early name in Acts: the Way. Before "Christian" became common speech, Luke remembers the movement as a path—an embodied manner of life, a walk. That label isn't a break from Israel; it is Israel-language translated into the street Greek of the empire. A people who "walk" in God's ways now

11. Sproul, *John*, loc. 3533; see also John 14:9–11.

12. Davidson, *Moses Maimonides*, 299–315, 473–478.

confess that the Way has a face and a voice. Jesus does not merely point toward the road; He says, "*I am the way*" (John 14:6).

This is also why Jesus' invitation to take His yoke matters. "My yoke is easy," He says—not because it is thin, but because it is true (Matt. 11:30). He is not offering an anti-Torah religion; He is offering Messiah's yoke: covenant carried as mercy, obedience carried by the Spirit, discipleship unhooked from fear and spiritual performance. And that helps us read Acts 15 with sobriety.

When Peter protests the "yoke" that some wanted to place on Gentiles, he is not calling Judaism a burden. He is rejecting the demand that Gentiles must undergo full proselyte conversion—circumcision and the entire package—as the price of belonging. The Council refuses that yoke and instead gives a narrow set of baseline boundaries that makes shared life and shared table possible, while Moses is still read every Sabbath.[13] In other words: the nations enter Israel's story through a merciful gate, not by replacing Israel and not by being crushed under an imposed identity they were never commanded to bear.

Jesus and the Last Days: His Voice, Not Ours

Jesus lived with a clarity we often lack. He did not panic over the Last Days. He interpreted them through the mercy of God. His longest eschatological teaching—Matthew 24–25—reads less like a prophecy chart and more like a pastoral briefing.

When the disciples asked, "*Tell us, when will these things happen*?" He did not feed their fear. He steadied them. Do not be alarmed. The end is not yet. Do not be led astray. The point was not to make them clever about timelines, but faithful under pressure. His warnings were never theatrical threats; they were guardrails meant to keep a small, vulnerable community from being shattered by deception, violence, and despair.

And then He does something that should embarrass our modern sensationalism: He ties endurance to ordinary covenant faithfulness. He tells them how to live—how to carry themselves when the world becomes

13. On "the Way" as the early designation for the Jesus movement, see Acts 9:2; 19:9, 23; 22:4; 24:14, 22. On Jesus as "the Way," see John 14:6; and on Jesus' "easy yoke," Matt. 11:28–30. On the "yoke" controversy as the question of imposing full proselyte conversion (circumcision and the law as a requirement for Gentile inclusion), and on the Council's baseline prohibitions and ongoing synagogue context ("Moses . . . read every Sabbath"), see Acts 15:1–21.

unstable. Love enemies. Forgive without keeping score. Give bread. Welcome the stranger. Visit the prisoner. Pray. Watch. Endure. The great test, in His telling, is not whether you cracked a code; it is whether you stayed human—merciful, truthful, faithful—when fear offered you shortcuts. This is not a Jesus who recruits panic. This is a Jesus who refuses to let panic recruit His disciples.

Jesus as Israel's King and God's Presence

When He entered Jerusalem, He did not marshal an army. He came as Zechariah foretold: humble, riding on a donkey. He wept over the city that refused mercy. He did not curse Israel; He carried Israel's grief. He did not abandon His people; He bore their destiny.[14]

And when the crisis finally came, Jesus' greatest claim did not need pagan borrowing or philosophical cover. Alan Segal's work on the rabbinic "two powers" controversy (too often treated as a master key in popular reconstructions) helps us see why: the categories in question were already being contested within Jewish Scriptural interpretation—especially around enthronement and agency texts like Daniel 7.[15]

The pressure points were Jewish before they were philosophical. Jesus of Nazareth spoke in Israel's own Scripture-grammar—the Son of Man from Daniel's vision. Under oath and under pressure, He spoke the sentence that explains the ferocity of His accusers: the Son of Man would come with the clouds and would be seated at the right hand of Power.[16]

That is why the reaction was so severe. They did not hear a mere teacher predicting vindication. They heard a Galilean Jew placing Himself inside the throne room of Israel's God—claiming the authority of the

14. Zech. 9:9; Matt. 21:4–5 (cf. Mark 11:1–10; Luke 19:28–40; John 12:14–15); Luke 19:41–42; Matt. 23:37; Isa. 53:4 (cf. Matt. 8:16–17); 1 Pet. 2:24; Rom. 11:1–2.

15. Segal, *Two Powers in Heaven*, 209. On Segal's "two powers" thesis, later secondary treatments sometimes treat his argument as a ready-made metaphysical grid. I find Heiser's use of Segal to lean in that direction—useful in places as a provocation, but too confident as an organizing framework.

16. On Jesus' climactic "Son of Man" claim as a throne-room assertion within Israel's own Scriptural grammar, see Dan. 7:13–14 (the Son of Man "coming with the clouds" and receiving dominion), read alongside Psalm 110:1 ("Sit at my right hand")—a pairing widely recognized as shaping the trial-scene language in the Synoptic Gospels. For the Gospel accounts of the high priest's reaction (including the tearing of garments as a sign of perceived blasphemy), see Mark 14:61–64 (par. Matt. 26:63–66; Luke 22:69–71).

heavenly court, the right to sit down where no creature sits, and the destiny of the nations described in Daniel's dominion vision. The outrage was not confusion. It was recognition. His claim was not, "I have an idea." It was, "I have a seat"—not a seat stolen from God, but a seat that discloses how God turns His face toward the world.

Rome crucified Him as a failed Jewish rebel. God raised Him as Israel's vindicated Son of Man. The Resurrection was not a metaphor. It was not a myth. Historical work can do real service: it can clear away lazy caricatures, recover first-century texture, and show why Jesus' message made sense inside Israel's world.

But the same work also has limits. Our sources are partial, our reconstructions contested, and the "quest" can never deliver the kind of certainty modern people sometimes demand. That is not a failure of faith; it is a reminder about what history can and cannot do. In the end, the Resurrection is not a datum we possess the way we possess an artifact. It is by testimony based on eyewitnesses (see 1 Cor. 15).

It is God's act of vindication—God's yes to Jesus after the world's no. History can trace the contours of the claim and its early effects; it cannot finally contain the meaning of that vindication. That meaning belongs to theology—because vindication is not merely what happened, but what God has declared true.

It was God's yes to everything Jesus said and did:

- Yes to the poor.
- Yes to the merciful.
- Yes to the peacemakers.
- Yes to the persecuted.
- Yes to Israel's story.
- Yes to the nations being gathered in.
- Yes to the renewal of creation.

Jesus makes the Father known not through theory but through Presence. To meet Jesus is to meet what God is like—holiness without superiority, authority without coercion, truth without cruelty, kindness with backbone.

So, I do not need the distorted Jesus of medieval polemics or the confused Yeshu of later slanders or the political mascot of modern factions. I need the living face of the Father—the One who shows us that divine power is not the power to crush, but the power to heal; not the power to dominate, but the power to keep covenant.

- Mary sings His hope.
- James practices His wisdom.
- Jude guards His mercy.
- And Jesus fulfills the story they all cherished.

He is the center of the family story. He is the anchor of our eschatology. He is the One who stands at the end of the age and says, without melodrama and without distance: Do not be afraid. When we see Him clearly, everything else grows quiet (see Psalm 46:10).

Chapter 7—A Lost Sister Found at Jacob's Well

"The hour is coming, and is now here."

—John 4:23

"A wounded healer is the one who heals the world."

—A Jewish legend (as retold by Henri Nouwen)

Jesus never met a boundary He was unwilling to cross for the sake of love. In the middle of John's Gospel, He is tired, thirsty, and waiting at a well in Samaria—a region many Jews avoided, a wound carried in Israel's memory. The person He chooses to speak with is not a priest, not a scribe, not a respectable patron. It is a Samaritan woman—alone, exposed, and already used to being read as a problem rather than a person (see John 4:4–42).

Years ago, I often heard this story preached in an individualistic, evangelistic key—almost as a moral warning. But no rabbi speaks the way Jesus speaks if his aim is to shame. He tells her the truth without turning it into a spectacle. He names her life without making her life the point. And He invites her into a theological conversation that only someone formed by Scripture could sustain—treating her not as a cautionary tale, but as a serious interlocutor in Israel's hope.

Samaritans were not pagans.[1] They were family—estranged, wounded, misremembered.[2] And to this woman, Jesus reveals something He speaks with full clarity only a handful of times:

"*I who speak to you am he*" (John 4:26).

I am the Messiah.

This is not a footnote in the Gospel. It is the hinge. The story turns here—at a well, in disputed territory, through a woman the world had taught to keep her eyes down.

The Scandal of Wanting to Be like the Nations

To feel the weight of Samaria, we must name a scandal that begins long before Jews and Samaritans didn't get along. Israel was called to be different—not by superiority, but by covenant. Their life was meant to show that the God of Abraham can dwell with human beings: governing not through spectacle or coercion, but through Torah-shaped justice, restraint, mercy, and worship.

Then comes the request that still reads like heartbreak: "*Give us a king . . . like all the nations.*" It wasn't merely a leadership question. It was a spiritual craving—Israel asking for the kind of security the surrounding peoples trusted. Samuel hears it as rejection. God names it as rejection too—not of Samuel, but of the Lord's own kingship (1 Sam. 8:4–22).

That "*like the nations*" desire does something subtle. It turns covenant into competition. It trains people to look for salvation in centralization, muscle, and managed outcomes. It makes fear feel wise (1 Kings 12; 2 Kings 17). Yes, God will use the monarchy. But Scripture is unsparing about what imitation produces: the burden increases, compromises multiply, and eventually the house divides. Samaria is what that division looks like when it becomes an inherited wound—political, religious, and familial all at once.

Jacob's Daughter at Jacob's Well

The woman at the well is not confused about who she is.

1. Purvis, *Samaritan Pentateuch and the Origin of the Samaritan Sect*, 87–103.
2. Pummer, *Samaritans*, 36–46, 128–41.

- She knows Jacob.
- She knows the well.
- She knows the feud.
- She knows the question that never goes away.
- Her argument about mountains isn't geography. It's belonging.[3]

Jacob's well is not just a water source; it is a marker of inheritance—an old, stubborn sign that this land and this family story go back to the patriarchs. And yet here, at the shared origin, the fracture remains: competing sanctuaries, competing memories, competing claims about where the God of Israel will set His Name.

"Where is the place God will make His Name dwell?"

Jesus answers her with a phrase that unlocks the horizon of Scripture:

"*The hour is coming, and is now here*" (John 4:23).

Not someday only.

Not "escape first."

Not "wait until conditions are perfect."

The barriers are falling. The family is widening. The Father is seeking worshipers—people who will worship in spirit and truth because God Himself has drawn near. Jesus is not trying to win an argument. He is rebuilding a world—starting with a woman no one expected God to seek.

The Gospel Spreads Through Wounds

She leaves her jar—the small emblem of her daily burden—and runs home with the simplest sermon ever preached:

"*Come, see a man . . .*" (John 4:29).

And they come.

And they listen.

And they believe.

3. On Jacob/Shechem inheritance-memory behind "Jacob's well," see Gen. 33:18–20; Gen. 48:22; Josh. 24:32, alongside John 4:5–6, 11–12.

The Gospel moves this way: through people who have been seen without being consumed, corrected without being crushed, restored without being managed. It moves through those who suddenly realize that God was seeking them long before they ever thought to seek Him.

Here Jesus stands fully within His Jewish world: healing divided Israel, restoring forgotten Israel, and opening Israel's hope to the nations—not through coercion, but through mercy. And this is where the language of restoration starts to glow in the background—language we will need in the next chapter. Watchmen calling Ephraim back to Zion and a Netzar (branch) rising from a cut-down stump. Jesus is not inventing a new story at Jacob's well. He is stepping into Israel's old story at the place where it hurts and announcing that the hour of repair has arrived.

Messiah as Moshiach—and the Samaritan Taheb

One final detail illuminates the entire encounter. When the Samaritan woman says "Messiah," she is not speaking only in the register many of us assume. John glosses the term: *Messias, which is called Christ*—the Greek Christos likewise meaning "anointed." The word naturally leans toward Israel's royal and priestly world and for many Jews toward a Davidic horizon.

But Samaritans carried a distinct accent of hope based on Torah. Their expected deliverer was often described as *the Taheb—the Restorer*—a prophet-like-Moses figure who would set worship right and heal what had been divided. That is why the woman's words lean Moses-ward: "*When he comes, he will tell us all things.*"[4]

Messianic hope was never monolithic in Israel. Jesus meets people inside the longing they carry—not dismissing it, not flattening it, but fulfilling it. In this one encounter, the horizons touch: David's promise of an anointed king, and Moses' promise of a truth-speaking restorer. And Jesus reveals Himself without forcing her vocabulary to become someone else's.

He gives her living water first. Then He gives her a name for what her heart has been waiting for.

A. B. Simpson Saw This Before We Did

Christ the Savior, who meets the shamed without shaming them.

4. Pummer, *Samaritans*, 135–141.

Christ the Sanctifier, who reorders worship away from rivalry and toward truth.

Christ the Healer, who closes a wound of centuries in a single conversation.

Christ the Coming King, who reveals His identity not in Jerusalem's courts but at Jacob's well.

Perhaps this is a new way of reading Simpson's presentation of what he coined as the *Fourfold Gospel*. But it is my way of emphasizing how Simpson was already pushing back against the emerging extreme individualism of modernity into our contemporary era. The Gospel begins with persons, yes, but it never begins with isolated persons. It begins with a people, a household, an *edah* gathered by mercy. That is why Interlude 1 matters: "*Behold your mother*" is spoken to the disciple whom Jesus loved, but it is not merely a private moment between two individuals. It is a communal word—Jesus forming a family at the foot of the cross.

Even the title we habitually use—the Samaritan woman—carries baggage. At best, it can mean "the one is not like us," but even then, it subtly diverts the story from the Abrahamic covenant, as if the scene were mainly about an outsider's inclusion rather than the Messiah's repair of a covenant-family wound. In the fourth Gospel, both the woman at Jacob's well and the beloved disciple function as doorways for the reader: you are being addressed, and you are being placed inside a renewed people. At the well, she is not treated as a religious consumer or a psychological case study; she is encountered as a representative person through whom an estranged community is opened, gathered, and repaired. If we miss the communal dimension, we will miss what John 4 is really doing—and we will also miss why Simpson's *Fourfold Gospel* has more depth than a slogan.[5]

What Simpson, a son of the Scottish diaspora to Canada—formed in the Princetonian-era Presbyterian world—grasped was not a slogan but a shape: Jesus moves toward the wounded edges without cutting Himself off from Israel's root-story. He could preach a Gospel expansive enough to heal and to send yet anchored enough to resist becoming a mere religious mood or a national program. His instinct was apostolic: mercy that goes outward, covenant that stays rooted, and mission that refuses to sever itself from the Scriptures that first named the Messiah.

5. Simpson, "Aggressive Christianity," 260–62; Simpson, *Christ in the Bible: Joshua*, ch. 5, "Thirty-One Kings, or the Victory Over Self," section "Selfish Prayers."

And yet this very strength could be misunderstood. Simpson's simplicity inspired countless individual evangelists, but in some streams, it also contributed—unintentionally—to a pattern in which proclamation became a common platform detached from the embodied evidence of the Gospel in-deed: mercy practiced, wounds tended, communities formed, and the poor remembered.[6]

That is why the standard caricature misses him. Simpson is often filed away as a merely individual revivalist—an untethered Keswick "holiness" enthusiast, even a faith-healer with a thin theology. Part of that misreading is temperamental: much modern evangelical (and especially modern Reformed) polemical evaluation operates by isolating individual doctrinal criteria—assurance, interiority, "higher life" claims, models of sanctification, and a quasi-automatic account of perseverance grounded in election—criteria that are not always irrelevant but are often beside the point and can easily divert attention from the communal and missional form a theology actually generates.

Simpson's center of gravity was not a private spirituality refined for the already-saved, but a Christ-shaped life meant to form a people: worship reordered away from rivalry, mercy embodied in public, and mission carried outward without severing itself from Israel's root-story.

A good deal of the "Simpson-as-untethered-perfectionist" caricature comes downstream of B. B. Warfield's polemical taxonomy. In *Perfectionism*, Warfield places A. B. Simpson within the late nineteenth-century "higher life" stream and flags him for the "extravagance" of his theories and the breadth of his influence—language that has often shaped how later readers label Simpson before they read him. Warfield's category-mapping is not useless, but it can obscure Simpson's center of gravity: a Christ-shaped theology ordered toward mission, not a free-floating holiness scheme or healing subculture.[7]

Simpson was closer to the opposite: a theologian of mission whose spirituality was disciplined by Scripture, ordered toward the nations, and integrated into a coherent Christ-centered vision. Whatever excesses later attached themselves to his movement, Simpson himself was trying to hold together what evangelicals often split apart—deeper life and costly

6. Banzhaf, "Diaspora Movement through A. B. Simpson," 39–47.

7. Warfield, *Perfectionism*, vol. 2, "The 'Higher Life' Movement," loc. 6882 (discussion of "Albert B. Simpson"); see also Warfield, *Perfectionism*, vol. 2, "The Victorious Life," locs. 7351–7382, where Warfield engages Simpson's teaching in the context of his broader critique of perfectionist/higher life trajectories.

obedience, healing and holiness, urgency and patience, experience and covenantal grounding—so that the Gospel would not only be preached but embodied and carried to the world.

Bernie Van De Walle's work on Simpson helps here, because it presents the Fourfold Gospel as a lived, Christ-centered synthesis—missionary at its core, not a doctrinal poster on a wall or a set of slogans. At the same time, it bears the imprint of its nineteenth-century setting and its characteristic theological instincts as Simpson also leaned into the evangelical diversity of his era—drawing from multiple streams without surrendering his center in Christ and mission.[8]

And yet, in its best applications, its strength is precisely its breadth: it holds together Savior, Sanctifier, Healer, and Coming King as one integrated Gospel rhythm. In our recent global gatherings, Bernie has pressed that point persuasively treating the Fourfold Gospel not as nostalgic branding, but as a comprehensive pattern for worship, formation, and mission.

And when it comes to the Coming King, Franklin Pyles is even more direct: for Simpson, eschatology was not trivia or prediction-talk—it was the engine of holiness and mission, the hope that propelled a people to "bring back the King" by carrying the Gospel outward.[9]

For Simpson, the Messiah's mission always moved outward: from Israel's rooted center to the wounded edges of the world. John 4 gives us a first living picture of that movement: the Messiah gathering forgotten branches of Abraham's family at Jacob's well without ever severing Himself from the tree that gave Him life.

Paul L. King captures Simpson's Kingdom logic with a phrase that fits John 4 perfectly: "*the overlapping of the ages*"—the Kingdom is "here now, but not fully here yet." In other words, Jesus gives real foretastes (living water, repaired worship, healed wounds) without pretending the story is finished. We live in the "border zone": tasting the powers of the age to come while still waiting for the King's full appearing.[10]

Recent Alliance scholarship reinforces this same vision. Peter R. Laughlin's essay, "*Reframing Missionary Eschatology for the Global Alliance*," argues that the early Christian and Missionary Alliance never separated its missional energy from its eschatological hope; Simpson's mission practice and end-time horizon were intertwined rather than competing.

8. Van De Walle, *Heart of the Gospel*, loc. 560.

9. Pyles, "Missionary Eschatology of A. B. Simpson," 29–47.

10. King, *Living in the Border Zone*, Kindle.

In Laughlin's telling, "the Coming King" was not an end-times hobby or an anxiety engine—it was the horizon that gave courage, patience, and urgency to the work of witness, compassion, and church planting.

Laughlin also frames his argument as a fresh hearing of Franklin Pyles's concern raised nearly 40 years earlier: the point is not to rebrand Simpson or to baptize a nineteenth-century template as timeless, but to retrieve The Alliance's original *shape*—an eschatology that keeps the Church outward-facing. Read this way, proclaiming the Gospel is not a flight from the world but participation in God's promised repair of it: the Spirit forms a people who embody mercy in advance of the Kingdom, even as they announce the King. That is the summons to renewal: hope that does not evacuate history, but steadies the Church to endure, to serve, and to speak with clarity when fear and speculation are louder than faith.[11]

Torat Edom and the Healing at the Well

What happens at Jacob's well is more than a personal conversion. It is a public sign of Torat Edom—a lens that rises from the wound and how Jesus of Nazareth fulfills this and shows how the wound is healed.

Samaria was one of Israel's deepest fractures, a scar running back to the divided kingdom and the long afterlife of exile. But Jesus does not avoid the fracture. He walks straight into it.

Torat Edom names this movement: Messiah restoring estranged branches of Abraham's family—not by erasing distinctions, and not by demanding uniformity, but by reconciling what history has trained us to treat as permanent division.

In the Samaritan woman, we see the first sign of promised repair: Jacob and the estranged house meeting again, not through force, but through living water offered with tenderness.

Here the Messiah begins mending the oldest fractures of the covenant family.

A Bridge We Often Miss

Samaria was not the only branch of Abraham living on the margins of Jewish memory. Arabia lived there too. Both Samaritans and the

11. Laughlin, "Reframing Missionary Eschatology for the Global Alliance," 249.

descendants of Ishmael carried partial memories of God—wounded histories, half-remembered covenants, longings not for dominance but for recognition.[12] Jesus goes through Samaria, not around it. That pattern matters. The Gospel does not advance by treating wounded peoples as obstacles. It advances by entering wounds without contempt—by offering living water rather than rivalry.

Centuries later, Islam would preserve echoes—sometimes faint, sometimes striking—of biblical memory: the God who sees the outcast, reverence for Mary and Jesus, the ache for cleansing and mercy.[13] Not theological agreement, but a recognizable human hunger.

John 4 gives the posture: speak truthfully, refuse fear, and offer what only Messiah can give.

The Samaritan woman is not a side character in the Gospel story; she is an early window into its shape. At Jacob's well, Jesus does not bypass Israel's fractures—He enters them to restore a sister. He names what is broken without shaming the broken. He offers living water as covenant mercy, not as spiritual escape. And He reorders worship away from rivalry and toward truth: a people formed by the Father's initiative, gathered by the Son, and animated by the Spirit.

I should say this plainly: nothing in this book is meant to drift into an anti-Trinitarian reading. John 4 is already triune in its own grammar—the Father seeks worshipers, the Son speaks the truth that unveils the Father, and the Spirit is the mode of real worship ("in spirit and truth"). The God who hovered over the waters in the beginning is the same God who draws near in the Word made flesh and the same God who indwells and empowers the people He gathers. I am not reducing God to a scheme; I am naming the biblical pattern of His nearness.

He comes near to restore a sister. He names what is broken without shaming the broken. He offers living water as covenant mercy, not as spiritual escape. That is why she can stand here as the first missionary of the restored assembly. She becomes a first sign of the community Jesus is forming: rooted in Israel's story, open to the nations, centered on living water, healed by mercy, courageous in testimony, and unafraid of the

12. Firestone, *Journeys in Holy Lands,* on Islamic memory-work around Abraham/Ishmael traditions; see also Gen. 16–21 for the Ishmael narratives as a biblical root-layer, 23–104.

13. Griffith, *Bible in Arabic,* on biblical memory in Islamic contexts; for Qur'anic reverence for Mary and Jesus, Qur'an 3:45–49; 19:16–36.

future. She is a first branch reaching outward—an early hint of the vine that will one day span the world.

And she sharpens the next question. If Jesus is healing Israel's fracture at Jacob's well, what does it mean that the earliest public name attached to His movement is *Nazōraioi*—with its echoes of *branch* and *watchmen* language inside Israel's own Scriptures? The answer takes us from a well in Samaria to the roads of empire where the Gospel must be spoken in public without becoming captive to any nation. That is where Paul enters—not as the inventor of a new religion, but as the emissary of Israel's Messiah to the nations: the lived meaning of Israel as relationship.

Interlude 3—Israel as Relationship: the Apostle Paul

"For I could wish that I myself were accursed and cut off from Messiah for the sake of my brothers, my kinsmen according to the flesh. They are Israelites . . ."

—Romans 9:3–4

"To bring about the obedience of faith among all the nations . . . to the only wise God be glory through Jesus the Messiah."

—Romans 1:5; 16:26 (paraphrased)

By the time we reach Jude, the family story feels like it is closing in: Mary has sung, James has shepherded, and Jude is contending. It is tempting to assume the New Testament now pivots away from Israel's internal life toward a gentile future. For many of us, Paul becomes the turning point—either the great liberator from Jewish religion or, from the opposite angle, the man who invented Christianity. Both readings are wrong.

If Jude is the last voice of Jesus' brothers and James is the halakhic anchor at the center of the family, then Paul is not the founder of a different project. He is the diaspora brother-in-law shaped by the same Scriptures, seized by the same Messiah, ordered into the same mission, but sent out along the outer roads of empire. James keeps the house in order. Jude guards the doors and the memory. Paul carries the same story down the highways of the nations.

And the world in which they all work is not Israel the modern nation-state, but Israel as covenant life—Israel as qahal and edah: a summoned assembly and a witnessing people. If we miss that, we will misread almost everything Paul says about the Last Days.

At this point a clarification matters, because modern Christian language often fails us. When I say, "relationship over religion," I am not rejecting religion itself. True religion is the form that protects the fire: it gives shape to devotion and keeps relationship from dissolving into sentiment. What I am rejecting is religion without relationship—faith reduced to easy *believism* and theology without encounter. The prophets never opposed religion; they opposed hypocrisy.

Micah's triad still stands—justice, mercy, and humble walking with God—and James names "pure and undefiled religion" as care for the vulnerable and a life unstained by the world. Jesus honored worship, Sabbath, and prayer, yet refused to let form replace love; He turned ritual into relationship and insisted, "I desire mercy, not sacrifice" (see Mic. 6:8; Jas. 1:27; Hos. 6:6; Matt. 6:5–6, 9:13, 12:7, 15:8–9; Mark 2:27).

Israel Before Borders: Qahal and Edah

Long before there was a map called Israel, there was a people called Israel standing at Sinai, hearing a Voice that bound them to Himself. Qahal names the gathered assembly summoned by that Voice; edah names the witnessing community that carries that revelation forward. In that sense, Israel is a religion before it is a regime: a pattern of worship, memory, law, mercy, and mission—a family shaped by covenant, not merely by territory.[1]

Yes, Scripture can speak of *goy* and *am* (nation and people). Yes, there is land and kingdom and border, but when the prophets warn and woo, the Israel they address is not a flag; it is a people who have forgotten how to live before the Face of God. James, Jude, and Paul never leave that world behind. When Paul speaks of "Israel," "the fathers," "the covenants," "the adoption," "the promises" (see Rom. 9:4–5), he is speaking of this covenantal Israel—entrusted with the oracles of God, called to be a light to the nations, and judged when that light becomes a weapon rather than a lamp.

1. On Israel as qahal and edah (assembly and witnessing community) and its continuity into the New Testament see the standard lexical work Schmidt, "ekklesia" in *Theological Dictionary of the New Testament*, and the biblical foundations in Deut. 4:10, 9:10; Num 20:4; Ps 22:22, 25.

Stephen stands exactly on this fault line. In Acts 7, he does not preach a new religion; he rehearses the story of Israel-before-borders—Abraham called while still in Mesopotamia, Joseph sent ahead into Egypt, Moses meeting the Holy One on Gentile soil where even Midian becomes "holy ground." His sermon is a qahal/edah manifesto: the God of the tent and the wilderness, the God who precedes temple and territory, still calling a people to hear and to bear witness.

It is no accident that Saul/Paul is there, guarding the cloaks while Stephen is stoned. The young pharisee is not merely offended by blasphemy; he is suspicious of this Jesus-movement way of telling Israel's story—this reading that loosens the grip of land and shrine and dares to claim that the Crucified One is the true Temple. The irony is severe and beautiful: the very man who watches Stephen die will become the apostle who most clearly articulates the same vision—Israel as qahal and edah, entrusted with covenantal light now breaking outward toward the nations.

Before the world ever heard the word "Christian," Acts will later call this Jesus movement "the sect of the Nazōraioi" (see Acts 24:5). Chapter 8 will open it fully—and will show why even the question "Can anything good come out of Nazareth?" carries more weight than we usually hear.

Paul's Conversion: Not Out of Judaism, but Deeper Into Israel's Calling

On the Damascus Road, Paul does not discover a new religion. He discovers that the God of Abraham has already acted in Israel's story by raising the crucified Messiah and enthroning Him as Lord of all. That revelation does not move him out of Israel. It throws him farther in.

He still calls Israel "*my brothers, my kinsmen according to the flesh.*" He still speaks of "our fathers." He still regards the Temple, covenants, and promises as real—not as metaphors to be spiritualized away. What changes is this: Paul sees that Israel's vocation is now pressing outward toward the nations in the way Isaiah and the Psalms always foresaw. "*I have set you as a light for the nations . . .*" (see Isa. 49:6; Acts 13:47). The risen Jesus does not send Paul to start "Christianity." He sends him to do what Israel was always meant to do: make the God of Israel known to the nations without turning Israel into an empire. James, presiding in Jerusalem, and Paul, traveling the roads, are two expressions of one covenantal mission.

Israel as Religion, Not Modern Nation

Here is where our language easily betrays us. When many modern Christians hear "Israel," they immediately picture the modern state, a political project tangled in war and diplomacy, a prophetic symbol driving headlines and sermons. Paul never saw that world. James and Jude never preached into that world. They saw synagogues, Torah-shaped communities, diaspora Jews, God-fearers, and pagans groping after unknown gods. Sure, Rome was occupying, but life went on.

For them, "Israel as religion" does not mean a generic faith tradition. It means a people who know the Name, keep a calendar that rehearses redemption, read a Book that tells them who they are, and live by a Torah that trains them in justice, mercy, and humility. Paul's anguish in Romans 9–11 is not that Israel is losing a political project; it is that Israel as covenant people—Israel as the qahal of the living God—has only partially recognized the One to whom its entire story pointed.

"*To them belong the adoption, the glory, the covenants, the giving of the law, the worship, and the promises . . . from their race, according to the flesh, is the Christ*" (Rom. 9:4–5). Notice the verb: "belong"—present tense. Not "used to belong." Not "belonged until the Church arrived." Paul insists that Israel's religious vocation remains in force even as he preaches Messiah among the nations and the Jews as a subset of Israel.[2]

James, Jude, and Paul: Same Battle, Different Angles

Jude stands inside the house, protecting the edah from false teachers and false memories. James sits at the family table in Jerusalem, guiding the qahal with halakhic wisdom—listening to reports, weighing Scripture, discerning how Israel's covenant life embraces the nations. Paul stands outside the house, on the roads of empire, fighting the same forces in a broader arena.

They are contending with the same distortions: lawlessness dressed up as grace, gentile arrogance toward the Jewish root, and forgetfulness of Israel's vocation. All three refuse to let Israel's religion be hijacked—by fantasies that dissolve covenant into ideas, by imperialism that baptizes power as kingdom, or by ethnic pride that forgets mercy is the only ground of anyone's standing. Jude guards the Evangelion from being rewritten.

2. Staples, *Idea of Israel in Second Temple Judaism*, introduction, 3–4, 11; and ch. 1, 51.

James guards its practice from being corrupted. Paul guards it from being repackaged as a gentile possession.

To Save a Life

A great deal of modern "Paul talk" begins with an assumption: Paul expected Jesus back any minute—next season, next summer, in his own lifetime. There is almost a consensus of tone in historical Jesus studies: Paul sounds urgent. And from that urgency, many scholars build their conclusions.

Some turn that urgency into a verdict: the earliest Christians expected an imminent end, it didn't arrive on schedule, and the whole movement must therefore be explained as a kind of failed apocalypse. Albert Schweitzer—often hailed as the most forthright investigator of Jesus of Nazareth in the classic era of German higher criticism and a key influence on later scholarship (including in the intellectual lineage behind James Tabor)—gave this suspicion a memorable image: Jesus "throwing Himself upon the wheel of history." That picture became a template not only for Jesus, but for Paul and the apostolic mission.[3]

Later apocalyptic readings often sharpen the point: if Jesus and Paul spoke as though the decisive intervention of God was near, then delay becomes the problem that forces reinterpretation. And once "delay" becomes the master key, it is easy to exaggerate a wedge between Paul and the Jerusalem family—turning James and Jude into the guardians of one project and Paul into the inventor of another. That move is common in modern reconstructions, but it is not the only way to read the evidence—and in my judgment, it often overstates the fracture.[4]

Others try to soften it. Certain readings take the edge off, suggesting Paul didn't really mean *soon* the way it sounds, or that his urgency is mostly rhetorical, or that apocalyptic language is simply a symbolic register. You can find very different moves across the spectrum, and they often disagree sharply with each other. But they're still circling the same question: What do we do with Paul's urgency?

Here is my proposal: What if Paul's urgency is not primarily a calendar problem? What if we have misread his urgency because we have removed him from Israel as a religion—Israel as covenant life, synagogue life, table life, halakhic life, a people learning how to live faithfully under pressure?

3. Schweitzer, *Quest of the Historical Jesus*, 370–71.

4. Tabor, *Jesus Dynasty*, 259–271.

When Paul is read as if he were a detached theologian building a new system, every line becomes a brick in a finished wall. We end up treating him like a second canon inside the canon—like a new voice "written in stone," overpowering the rest of Scripture rather than serving it.

But Paul doesn't write like a man chiseling timeless propositions. He writes like a man performing triage. He reads less like a philosopher and more like something closer to Mishnah—not because he is rewriting rabbinic literature, but because he is doing what faithful Jewish teachers have always done when lives are on the line. He is trying to preserve covenant fidelity amid real danger, real confusion, and real suffering.

In Judaism, there is a name for this kind of priority: *pikuach nefesh*—the duty to save life.[5] Sometimes the faithful move is not the slow construction of a system, but the urgent rescue of a people. Read Paul through that lens and his "urgency" looks less like a failed countdown and more like covenant emergency: protect the flock, keep the Gospel from being hijacked, form communities that can survive the empire without becoming the empire, and anchor Gentiles in Israel's God without turning them into a replacement Israel.

That is why Paul can summarize his entire vocation—at the beginning and end of Romans—in a phrase that doesn't sound like private spirituality at all: "*To bring about the obedience of faith among all the nations*" (Rom. 1:5; 16:26).[6] This is covenant language. Faith is not vague optimism but loyal trust in Israel's God as revealed in Messiah. Obedience is not self-saving effort but embodied allegiance that takes concrete form in communities, habits, and ethics.

Paul is inviting them into Israel's way of life—not by turning them into ethnic Jews, but by grafting them into the same covenantal pattern: worship of the one God, honor for His Torah (rightly read), faith in His Messiah, and participation in His mission. That is why Acts 15 matters so much and why James had to speak before Paul could act. James retrieves a lawful way for the nations to share Israel's God without taking on the whole yoke Israel bears. Paul lives that decision out, forming assemblies of Gentiles attached to Israel's covenant life without erasing their ethnic and cultural distinctives. Israel, as religion, is expanded, not abolished.[7]

5. *Pikuach nefesh ("saving life") as halakhic duty, m. Yoma 8:6; b. Yoma 85a–b (Steinsaltz); and Shulchan Aruch, Orach Chaim 328:2.*

6. Wright, *Paul and the Faithfulness of God*, 824–847.

7. Nanos, *Mystery of Romans*, 16, Romans addressing gentile misperceptions of Israel/

The Doorway for the Nations

Here is the stage modern Christian language often forgets. The New Testament does not move directly from "pagan nations" to "Gentile Christianity." It moves through a covenant doorway—an in-between space where Gentiles turn from idols, learn Israel's story, and attach themselves to Israel's God with real moral accountability.

This is where the Hillelite posture matters. Beit Hillel represents a way of holding Israel's covenant life that can receive seekers without erasing Israel. In the late Second Temple world there were already Gentiles orbiting synagogue life—drawn to Israel's Scriptures and Israel's ethics. The question was whether that approach could be honored without turning conversion into a gatekeeping weapon, and without turning inclusion into lawlessness.

Acts 15 answers with startling realism. The apostles refuse the forced conversion-track as the entry requirement—and they also refuse to baptize pagan life as "grace." They articulate a threshold of fidelity, a first step out of idolatry and pagan table-culture, so that Gentiles can be welcomed as nations without being absorbed as replacements. In later Jewish terms, this stage is close to what will be called *ger toshav*—a resident outsider who turns from idols and binds himself to the basic moral demands of living among God's people. You do not need later terminology to see the shape: it is a covenantal landing pad for the nations.

James protects Israel's covenant integrity. Paul lives that decision out on the roads of empire. One speaks so the doorway is lawful; the other walks through it so the nations can enter. This is not "Israel abolished." It is Israel's vocation pressing outward in Messiah—mercy widening the family without stealing the inheritance.

Olive Tree, Not Exchange Program

When Paul reaches for an image to describe what is happening between Israel and the nations, he does not choose a relay race. He does not say Israel ran first, dropped the baton, and now the Church runs instead. He chooses a tree:

Jews, 34–36 gentile believers framed as "righteous gentiles" under synagogue/halakhic expectations, 47 synagogue setting/house-community context, 55 Acts 15 invoked as an operative halakhic baseline for gentile participation, and 73 discussion of the "learning curve" for gentiles apart from Jewish communal association.

> "*If some of the branches were broken off, and you, although a wild olive shoot, were grafted in among the others and now share in the nourishing root . . . do not be arrogant toward the branches*" (Rom. 11:17–18).

The root is Israel's covenant story. The tree is Israel's vocation in Messiah. The branches are Jews and Gentiles together—some natural, some grafted. History does not move from "Israel the religion" to "Church the religion." It moves from "Israel alone" to "Israel with the nations" in the same living tree. That is why substituting "church" wherever Paul says "Israel" is so dangerous: it turns Paul's olive tree into an exchange program and fuels the lie that God swapped out one people for another. Paul will not allow it.[8]

In the Latin West, one of the most consequential "turns" in how Christians imagined history came through Augustine—not because he invented Replacement Theology, but because he gave Christendom a durable way to *organize time* and to *explain Jewish persistence* inside a Christian empire. In *The City of God*, Augustine frames the church's life as pilgrimage through the *saeculum*: not an evacuation story, not a national destiny story, but two "cities" intermingled until God's final judgment. That long, linear horizon helped steady Christian imagination after Rome's shocks. But it also made it easier, over time, for Christians to treat history as "our" providential march—so that the church's public dominance could feel like the natural shape of God's plan rather than an always-contested temptation.[9]

That's where Augustine's legacy becomes double-edged sword for a book like this. Augustine also supplied what later scholars call a "Jewish witness" logic: Jews must not be eradicated, because their continued existence—often in dispersion—functions as a kind of living testimony to the Scriptures Christians read and to the God who speaks in Israel's history. He famously reads the Psalmic line, "*do not slay them . . . scatter them*" as providential: Jewish scattering becomes, in his interpretation, a means by which the biblical books are carried through the nations even by a people who does not confess Jesus as Messiah.[10] In practice, that "witness" logic could restrain extermination; it could also rationalize humiliation. Over centuries, the same framework hardened into a social script: Jews as the

8. Soulen, *God of Israel and Christian Theology*, 171–189.

9. Augustine, *City of God*, books XVIII–XIX.

10. Augustine, *City of God*, XVIII.46.

perpetual "wandering" people—tolerated, contained, and made into an object-lesson inside Christian triumph.[11]

This is where Torat Edom becomes more than a metaphor. When a Christian civilization learns to speak of Israel mainly as a theological instrument—useful for Christian proof but displaced from living vocation—then "Israel as covenant relationship" is quietly replaced by "Israel as a prop in our story." Augustine did not intend the later cruelty, but he helped set categories that could be weaponized once the church fused itself to empire and began to confuse providence with possession. That is why Paul's anguish in Romans 9–11 matters so much: Israel is not a discarded stage in a Christian drama. Israel remains Israel—beloved, covenanted, entrusted—while the nations are grafted in by mercy. Any Last Days teaching that turns Jews into permanent object-lessons or makes history into a Christian nation-project is already drifting into an Edomite posture: covenant turned into conquest and theology turned into permission.[12]

Paul's own story is a reminder that the apostolic mission unfolded in real borderlands, not in a classroom taxonomy. When Paul recounts his early escape, he says it happened in Damascus under "the ethnarch of King Aretas" (see 2 Cor. 11:32–33)—a political detail that pulls the Jesus movement immediately into the contested world of neighboring powers and jurisdictions. The nations are not an abstract category in Paul; they are the real, nearby peoples among whom Israel's calling must be lived without surrendering Israel's covenant identity.

Paul's Eschatology: Family, Not Charts

All this matters deeply for the prophecy confusion named earlier. When we treat Israel primarily as a modern nation-state and then build eschatology around its borders and battles, we quietly teach that the Last Days are a geopolitical chess match. The letters of James, Jude, and Paul say something very different. For them, the crisis is not "Which nation wins?" but whether Jew and Gentile together will embody the religion of Israel's God—the obedience of faith, the ethic of love, the humility of the cross, the hope of Resurrection—amid whatever nations rise and fall.

Israel as religious relationship judges every nation, including Rome in Paul's day, the modern State of Israel, the United States, and all our

11. Fredriksen, *Augustine and the Jews*, 240, 289.

12. Nirenberg, *Anti-Judaism*, 3,459.

alliances and enemies. When evangelicalism fuses itself to any nation—Jewish, American, or otherwise—it abandons the posture these brothers model: citizens of heaven whose deepest allegiance is to Israel's God and Israel's Messiah, not to any earthly regime.

In that sense, Israel functions less like a state project and more like a covenantal vocation—a particular calling that carries within it a universal moral claim on the nations down through the ages. Here Ben Abrahamsom translates Rabbi Benamozegh's language into "religious federalism," which helps name why this cannot be captured by any regime: Israel's covenant is distinct, yet it serves as guardian of a moral order meant for all humanity (Noahide obligation), which means Israel's God stands in judgment over every political-religious fusion, whether nationalist or imperial. Abrahamson's Contemporary Jewish "multi-covenant" vocabulary makes the same point in modern terms: one moral root, distinct covenant communities, and therefore a transnational ethic that no state can monopolize.[13]

And this is also where Paul's urgency becomes newly intelligible. If Paul believed the living God was forming communities of "obedience of faith" among the nations—communities grafted into Israel's story, trained in covenant loyalty, and prepared to endure suffering without becoming violent—then of course his letters would sound urgent. He is not writing chart commentary. He is fighting for the shape of a reconciled family in the middle of an empire that devours families just like today!

Read this way, Paul's teaching on the Last Days sounds less like a timetable and more like a family conversation. Creation groans. Israel groans. The nations groan. The Spirit groans with us. And what is God doing? Fulfilling His promises to Israel, welcoming the nations into Israel's covenant life, and reshaping humanity into a single reconciled family in Messiah.

Paul's calling makes sense when read as edah rather than replacement: a commissioned witness body sent among the nations, accountable to Jerusalem, not severed from it. For Paul, judgment is real; wrath is real; the day is real. But the center of gravity is reconciliation, not abandonment: "*God has consigned all to disobedience, that he may have mercy on all*" (Rom. 11:32). That is not a chart. It is worship—rising from a Jew who met his own Messiah and discovered that the religion of Israel is more merciful, and more demanding, than he ever knew.

13. Abrahamson, *Confrontation and Engagement*, 217, "multi-covenantism" and "religious federalism" are a common moral root with distinct communities branching from it, foregrounding the Noahide covenant as binding moral code for non-Jews.

Chapter 8—Who Were the Netzarim/ Notzrim?

"There shall come forth a shoot (netzer) from the stump of Jesse . . ."

—Isaiah 11:1

"For there shall be a day when the watchmen (notzrim) will call in the hill country of Ephraim: 'Arise, and let us go up to Zion . . .'"

—Jeremiah 31:6

"For we have found this man a plague . . . and is a ringleader of the sect of the Nazōraioi."

—Acts 24:5

In Interlude 3, I mentioned—without unpacking it—that the Book of Acts preserves a public label for the Jesus movement before "Christian" became common speech or mentioned at Antioch (see Acts 11:26): "the sect of the Nazōraioi" (see Acts 24:5). This chapter opens that name and its conflations.

It is not a throwaway insult. It sits inside Israel's Scriptures, hopes, and contested memories. It echoes *Netzer* (*shoot/branch*, see Isa. 11:1) and *Notzrim* (*watchmen/keepers*, see Jer. 31:6). And it also carries the bruises of history, because names that begin as confession can later become slurs.

That is why the Gospel's skeptical question—"*Can anything good come out of Nazareth*?"—lands with more than regional snobbery (John 1:46). It can function as a dismissal of the entire claim: that God's renewal would come from the place nobody respects; that the promised Branch would rise from what looked cut down and dead—yet would "*take root downward and bear fruit upward*" (2 Kings 19:30; cf. Isa. 11:1); and that watchmen would summon Israel back to Zion—not by violence, but by witness (see Jer. 31:6). And in later polemical climates, the line could also be heard as a broader dismissal: these keepers, these watchmen, are suspect for an accusation in the book of Kings.

So, we will do something simple and necessary: recover what this name meant before later conflations and caricatures reshaped it. Two of the most important layers come straight from Israel's Scriptures: Netzer and Notzrim. Isaiah speaks of a Netzer springing from the stump of Jesse—a fragile sign of Davidic renewal growing out of what looked like a dead tree. Long before creeds or Gentile theology, Jesus' earliest followers understood themselves as the community gathered around that Branch.

And "branch" is more than imagery. The Scriptures also speak of a coming *Tzemach*—a Branch who will execute justice, heal the fractured house of David, and restore kingship to covenant fidelity (see Jer. 23:5; Zech. 6:12). Early believers did not see their assemblies as religious clubs, but as extensions of Messiah's own life—shoots attached to the living Branch—bearing His character into the nations without replacing Israel.

Jeremiah then speaks of Notzrim calling from the hills of Ephraim, summoning the people to go up to Zion (see Jer. 31:6). And here, a small scribal detail matters more than modern readers realize. The Hebrew root behind *Notzrim* is *Natsar*: to guard, keep, preserve—(Strong's H5341). In Kings, the same word-field appears in the phrase *mimigdal notzrim*: "*from the tower of the watchmen*" (2 Kings 17:9; 18:8)—a watchtower, a boundary-post, a place of vigilance. The vowel pointing does not create a secret second word; it simply clarifies which word we are hearing: not Netzer but Notzrim. Whether spelled more "fully" or more "sparingly" in different witnesses, the sense remains steady: vigilance, guardianship, and covenant-keeping.

By the time we reach the Book of Acts, that word-field has become the first public label for the movement: a "sect of the Nazōraioi." In other words, the earliest name for Jesus' followers was rooted in this Scriptural story of branch and guardianship—renewal rising from what looked dead and watchmen calling the people home.[1]

The Double Edge of "Watchmen"

The name echoes across Jewish memory—in hints, fragments, blessings, and polemics—but its first meaning is more beautiful than many realize. In the Deuteronomistic history, the northern kingdom is remembered as a people meant to guard covenant life, yet instead they "*secretly did things that were not right against the LORD*" and went after other gods (2 Kings 17:9).[2]

And the narrator adds a line that almost reads like an aerial photograph of a compromised land: they built illicit worship-sites "*from the tower of the watchmen to the fortified city*"—as if the whole territory were dotted with keepers who were supposed to see and warn. And yet the irony is sharp: the very places built for "watchfulness" became places where worship could be hollowed out and described as evil before the LORD.

Readers raised on fundamentalist preaching sometimes remember phrases like "high places" and "under every green tree" as if Scripture were issuing bans on modern objects—sometimes even Christmas trees. But the prophets and historians are not policing botany or décor. They are naming places—shrines, groves, and high places—where covenant loyalty was traded for rival worship and the liturgies of assimilation. The point is not superstition; the point is fidelity. The tragedy is that a landscape meant for vigilance became a landscape dotted with alternative altars—religion performed, conscience quieted, and the heart drifting elsewhere.

Archaeology adds a sobering footnote to that biblical critique. At Tel Arad—an Iron Age Judahite shrine—chemical residue analysis on incense altars found frankincense on one altar and cannabis (likely resin burned with animal dung to release its psychoactive effect) on the other, suggesting that altered states could be deliberately sought in cultic practice all over the Holy Land.[3] In other words, the language of "keepers" can carry both calling and warning that watchfulness can be fidelity—or vigilance turned hollow, even chemically amplified, while the heart drifts from covenant truth.

1. Brown, *Birth of the Messiah*,180, 211–223.

2. https://www.wikinoah.org/en/index.php/Notzrim

3. Arie, Rosen, and Namdar, "Cannabis and Frankincense at the Judahite Shrine of Arad," 5–28.

Over time, that double edge allowed the word to pick up negative overtones and become a playground for word-games. "*Can anything good come out of Nazareth*?" can be heard not only as a jab at a backwater town but—especially in later polemical climates—as a wider dismissal: these "keepers," these "watchmen," are suspect.

Later "watchers" traditions in Enochian literature further muddied the waters, making it easier to hear Notzri as something deviant—or even fatalistic—rather than as a name resonant with Isaiah's Branch and Jeremiah's call to Zion. Jeremiah's Notzrim are plainly human watchmen—people calling people—yet later imaginations blurred categories, imported angelic "watcher" templates, and supplied polemics with extra fuel.[4]

But to be a netzar/notzri in the first century was not to "join a new religion." It was to belong to a Jewish remnant—faithful Israel, waiting for God to renew His covenant, gather His people, and heal the nations through mercy. Jeremiah's Notzrim are not celestial beings but human watchmen—guardians who stand on the heights and call Israel home: "Watchmen [*notzrim*] will call . . . '*Arise, let us go up to Zion*'" (Jer. 31:6). Later imagination sometimes blurred these registers—*watchmen/watchers/Notzrim*—and once that blur existed, polemical wordplay could treat "Notzri" as suspect rather than hear its biblical resonance with Isaiah's *Branch* (*netzer*, see Isa. 11:1). And because Second Temple "watchers" traditions (most famously in 1 Enoch 6–16) became part of the wider symbolic atmosphere, the overlap became easier to exploit: what began as a prophetic-human vocation ("watchmen") could be re-coded into an insinuation about suspect spirits ("watchers"). The result is a distortion of memory: the remnant-name is made to sound like a warning label, instead of a Scriptural echo of hope.[5]

The earliest Netzarim/Notzrim did not rally around Herod's court or the Temple aristocracy. They followed a crucified Davidic heir whose kingdom refused both Zealot violence and Herodian collaboration. By the time Paul is accused before Felix, the movement is already being sized up as a public problem to manage: Tertullus calls it "the sect of the Nazarenes" (Acts 24:5)—language of containment, not covenantal recognition. And when Paul is brought before Festus and then heard by Herod Agrippa II (see Acts 25–26), the same posture is simply scaled up. Agrippa, a Roman client king positioned between imperial rule, priestly politics, and popular

4. Heiser, *Unseen Realm*, and *Reversing Hermon*.

5. Nickelsburg, *1 Enoch 1*; 238–47, 267, 272–74; Stuckenbruck, *Myth of Rebellious Angels*, 82.

unrest, evaluates the Jesus movement less as a remnant to join than as a disturbance to assess, classify, and keep within bounds—especially in an era already haunted by the "many" rival claimants Jesus warned would come (see Matt. 24:5, 11, 24).[6]

In a world where Edom had been welded into Judea by force and then enthroned by Rome, the Netzarim/Notzrim embodied another way: covenantal mercy instead of coercion, testimony instead of propaganda, the true Branch instead of an imperial "King of the Jews."

Second Temple Life Was Covenant Life

Second Temple life is not best described as "many Judaisms" floating in an academic terrarium. The sources show Israel living a covenantal life amid neighbors, trade routes, alliances, and threats. In 1 Maccabees, Judas and Jonathan encounter the Nabataeans, who receive them peaceably and report on Israelite communities under siege east of the Jordan. That is covenant history in motion—Israel's internal faithfulness and Israel's external pressures—rather than a story about "religions evolving." This is the world of Mary, of James, of Jude, and of the early Jerusalem community—the world explored throughout this book.

Recovering the early name Netzarim/Notzrim is not an attempt to rebrand modern Messianic Judaism, nor to create distance from it. It is simply a historical framing that predates all modern categories. The earliest followers of Jesus represented varied expressions of Jewish faithfulness—from the Jerusalem Netzarim/Notzrim to later poverty-oriented streams remembered later under labels such as *Ebionim* (*poor ones*)—long before "Christianity" existed as a separate religious system.

By retrieving this older language, we honor the first-century Jewish world of Jesus without importing modern identity debates. It allows Christians, Jews, and even Muslims to engage the story on historical rather than denominational grounds. Rabbi Ben Abrahamson has pursued that kind of historically grounded, Abrahamic conversation for many years—often outside the spotlight—and I have seen the fruit of it in the way some Muslim interlocutors not only listen but meaningfully engage the sources rather than dismiss them.

6. Josephus, *Jewish War* 2.342–404.

The Netzarim/Notzrim Are Not "the Ebionites"

It is equally important not to flatten everything into one label. Netzarim/Notzrim (as a public label in Acts) and Ebionites (as a later heresy label) are not identical categories.[7]

By the second century, "Ebionite" had become a name used in Christian polemical catalogues for communities associated—rightly or wrongly—with Torah observance, resistance to Gentile ecclesiastical developments, and disagreements over Christology and authority. Some of these groups may preserve genuine early trajectories; others may reflect later reactions and fractures. Either way, we must be careful: what we possess today is largely the description of opponents, not a full archive of self-representation.

However earnest their commitments, these later formations did not necessarily preserve the living Jerusalem family memory of Mary, James, Jude, or the Desposyni (Jesus' relatives). Recovering the word *Notzrim* is therefore not a return to Ebionitism but to something earlier and more basic: the Jewish remnant that first recognized in Jesus the Branch of Isaiah.

And let me be frank. The very word "Ebionite" also shows how thoroughly the "victors" can rewrite a story. What may have begun as a humble self-designation—ha-'evyonim, "the poor ones," beloved in the Psalms and echoed in the Beatitudes—reaches us largely through the shorthand of heresy catalogues: Irenaeus, Origen, Eusebius, Epiphanius, and their heirs. They did not simply describe a movement; they rebranded it.[8]

Some patristic writers even speak as if there were a founder named "Ebion," a move many modern scholars interpret as a back-formation—an explanatory fiction generated from the label itself rather than a real biographical origin.[9] The result is predictable: a Torah-keeping Jewish remnant that clung to Jesus as Messiah while remaining inside Israel's covenantal world gets turned into a cautionary tale. "Ebionite" becomes shorthand not for "the poor whom God blesses," but for the losers and dropouts of Christian history. In doing so, they did what empire always does: silence the local tongue, rename the village, and then quote themselves as the only reliable map.

7. Pritz, *Nazarene Jewish Christianity*, introduction, 19–70.

8. Luomanen, *Recovering Jewish Christian Sects and Gospels*, 241–42.

9. Bauckham, *Jude and the Relatives of Jesus in the Early Church*, 74–75.

Misunderstood by History

Moreover, over time, Netzarim/Notzrim acquired new meanings. As Christianity spread—often with imperial and later colonial force—it came to be associated in many Jewish memories not with the Branch of Isaiah, but with domination. Focusing in on the use of term Notzri in rabbinic and medieval sources often marked a religious "other" who could be dangerous.

Plus: Kings and Jeremiah are the daily bread of a Jew studying the Tanakh seriously; the "keeper/watchman" word-field is not exotic trivia but living text. In modern Hebrew and used in the State of Israel, *Noẓrî* typically means simply *Christian*, and the word can carry mixed memory: curiosity, distance, and for many, a lingering pain. The negative baggage is there.

This is not necessarily a rejection of Jesus Himself. It is often a response to what "Christian" came to represent in Jewish history: persecution, forced conversion, displacement, and polemics sanctified as piety. Understanding this helps Christians respond with humility rather than defensiveness. It invites us to ask not, "Why won't they accept our label?" but "What did we do with it?"

Labels are never neutral once they are weaponized. In our own day, Christian families in parts of Iraq and Syria had their houses marked with the Arabic letter *nūn* (ن) to identify them as "Nazarenes"—not for dialogue, but for demarcation, intimidation, and dispossession. In the aftermath, that same letter spread widely online as a symbol of solidarity, a reminder that names can be used either to target or to protect.

Nazir and Netzar: A Necessary Distinction

Because the terms sound alike, many readers instinctively fuse *Nazirite* and *Netzar* into one idea. They are not the same word, and they are not the same category. Nazirite (nazir) belongs to the vocabulary of consecration—a voluntary vow of being "set apart" (see Num. 6).

Netzarim/Notzrim, by contrast, lives in the orbit of n-ṣ-r : the resonance of Netzer ("branch/shoot," see Isa. 11:1) and the sense of guarding/keeping. The similarity is mostly a later sound-alike that can mislead modern ears, especially when Greek and English flatten the distinctions.

At the same time, the overlap is still real at the level that matters for this book: both sit inside Israel's embodied covenant world, where holiness is not an abstraction but a practiced loyalty. The earliest Jesus followers were not a free-floating "new religion." They moved inside the Torah-and-Temple ecosystem in which vows—including Nazirite vows—were a known form of devotion.

That shared world helps explain why Matthew's "Nazarene" language can function as a prophetic signal without turning Jesus into a Nazirite or the Netzarim into a vow-sect. The fuller logic—and why this word-field matters for how the Nazōraioi were heard, named, and contested—will be unpacked in the next chapter, including the question of whether Jesus Himself ever took (or honored) vow practices in that world.

Recovering the First Meaning

The original Netzarim/Notzrim were: Jews who believed the Messiah had come, a family formed around Jesus' teaching, a remnant faithful to the story of Israel, and a community that welcomed Gentiles through God's mercy—not through ethnic erasure or abandonment of Torah's story.

- They never stopped being Jews.
- They never abandoned Israel's Scriptures.
- They embodied the fulfillment of them.

If Mary reveals the heart of Israel, James its faithfulness, and Jude its courage, then the Netzarim/Notzrim reveal Israel's continuity—the Branch reconnecting the ancient root to the nations. In their confession that Yeshua is the Netzer of Isaiah, they help us see that HaShem's revelation and mission have a proper lineage: from Abraham, Isaac, and Jacob; through Moses, the prophets, and David; into the household of Mary and Joseph; and out through a Jewish remnant to the ends of the earth. "*There is no other name given under heaven given among men by which we must be saved*" (Acts 4:12).

Isaiah 11 does more than give us a messianic title. The Netzer from Jesse's stump is described as One who "*shall not judge by what his eyes see, or decide disputes by what his ears hear, but with righteousness he shall judge the poor, and decide with equity for the meek of the earth*" (Isa. 11:3–4).

That is a quiet but devastating critique of how religious people so often relate to one another. Much of Jewish–Christian history has been shaped by precisely the opposite pattern: judging one another by what we see—external forms, polemical snapshots, political alignments—and by what we hear—rumors, accusations, distorted retellings—rather than by the slow, covenantal listening Isaiah attributes to the Branch.

If the early Notzrim were those who gathered around this Netzer, then to bear His name faithfully today means learning His way of judgment. We are not free to let headlines, inherited grievances, or one-sided stories define "the Jews," "the Christians," or "the Muslims." The Branch refuses that kind of shallow seeing and hearing. His justice is oriented toward the poor and the meek—the ones most easily erased by our narratives—and it moves toward repair.

To stand under His banner is to let Him retrain our eyes and ears so that discernment becomes an instrument of reconciliation rather than a weapon in old religious feuds. To be Nazarenes today cannot mean clinging to our old hostilities or denominationalism. It means learning to see through His way of judging: not by what we think we see, not by what we have heard about "them," but by a righteousness that remembers the wounded and the overlooked. The Branch does not erase difference; He restores justice and makes reconciliation possible.

A Wider Family than We Remember

As Christianity grew into an imperial force, it not only forgot its Jewish roots; it also learned to treat another branch of Abraham's family as a permanent rival. The descendants of Ishmael—named in various early Jewish and Christian sources with biblical family-language (Hagarenes/Hagarites, Ishmaelites, Nabateans and related labels)—were never meant to be enemies of the covenant. Scripture blesses them, names them, and grants them a divinely promised destiny.

Yet for centuries, Christians often approached Muslims not as relatives carrying their own ancient memory of Abraham's God, but as theological competitors to be subdued. This, too, belongs to the amnesia the Netzarim/Notzrim help us confront.[10]

Jesus never trained His followers to despise the children of Ishmael. In the Gospels, He commands love of enemies and prayer for persecutors (see

10. Ishmael, Esau, and the wider Abrahamic horizon. For Ishmael's blessing and Esau's linkage to Ishmael's line within the wider Abrahamic family story, see Gen. 16–17; 21:8–21; 25:29–34; 26:34–35; 28:6–9; 33:1–11; 36:1–3. For contemporary engagement from Jewish Halakah, see Abrahamson and Al Sadiqin publications.

Matt. 5:43–45). He announces that *"many will come from east and west and recline at table with Abraham, Isaac, and Jacob"* (Matt. 8:11). He commends the faith of non-Israelites—the Roman centurion (see Matt. 8:5–13), the Syrophoenician/Canaanite woman (see Mark 7:24–30; Matt. 15:21–28), the Samaritan leper (see Luke 17:11–19)—and He makes a despised Samaritan the hero of His most famous parable (see Luke 10:25–37).

All of this sits comfortably inside the earlier biblical witness about Ishmael. God does choose Isaac as the covenant line, but He never abandons Ishmael:

- The angel of the LORD promises Hagar: *"I will surely multiply your offspring so that they cannot be numbered for multitude,"* and tells her to name the boy Ishmael, *"because the LORD has listened to your affliction"* (Gen. 16:10–11).
- God tells Abraham: *"As for Ishmael, I have heard you; behold, I have blessed him and will make him fruitful and multiply him greatly . . . I will make him into a great nation"* (Gen. 17:20).
- When Hagar and Ishmael are sent away, God hears the boy's cry, reassures Hagar, and is with Ishmael as he grows up (see Gen. 21:17–20).

If the Father blesses, hears, and is "with" Ishmael, the Son is not going to school His disciples in contempt for Ishmael's children. Instead, Jesus sends His followers "to the ends of the earth" (Acts 1:8)—which must eventually include deep, patient, truthful engagement with the Ishmaelite and Arab world and their often-persecuted Christian neighbors who also use Allah as the name for God in their Bibles.

So, Esau's story helps deepen the picture. He begins badly: despising his birthright for a bowl of stew (see Gen. 25:29–34) and marrying Hittite wives, which "made life bitter for Isaac and Rebekah" (see Gen. 26.34–35). From a covenant standpoint, he is doing exactly what Abraham warned against—binding the line of promise to the local Canaanite peoples (see Gen. 24:3). Rebekah's complaint is explicit: "I loathe my life because of the Hittite women" (Gen. 27:46).

But the text also shows Esau paying attention. When Jacob is blessed and sent to Paddan-aram to take a wife from his mother's family, Isaac frames the command precisely as not taking a Canaanite wife (see Gen. 28:1–2). Then we read:

> *Now Esau saw that Isaac had blessed Jacob and sent him away to Paddan-aram . . . and that as he blessed him he directed him, 'You must not take a wife from the Canaanite women,' and that Jacob had obeyed his father and his mother . . . So, when Esau saw that the Canaanite women did not please Isaac his father, Esau went to Ishmael and took as his wife, besides the wives he had, Mahalath the daughter of Ishmael, Abraham's son, the sister of Nebaioth.*
>
> —Genesis 28:6–9

Later she is called Basemath, daughter of Ishmael, sister of Nebaioth (see Gen. 36:3). Beneath the name-shift, the point is clear: Esau, seeing his parents' grief, intentionally seeks a wife from Abraham's wider family—through Ishmael. That is not nothing. Is it full repentance? The text does not sermonize. But it is at least a covenantal course-correction: a move away from Hittite/Canaanite lines and back toward Abraham's household. And that turn toward Ishmael's line is followed by one of the most moving reconciliation scenes in Scripture: "*But Esau ran to meet him and embraced him and fell on his neck and kissed him, and they wept*" (Gen. 33:4)

The Esau who once planned to kill Jacob (see Gen. 27:41) instead runs, embraces, kisses, and weeps. He initially refuses Jacob's gifts ("*I have enough, my brother*"; Gen. 33:9), then accepts them as a sign of restored relationship (see Gen. 33:11). Whatever future conflict will emerge between Israel and Edom, at the level of the brothers themselves, Genesis closes the loop with reconciliation, not hatred.

Put together—Esau's marriage into Ishmael's line (see Gen. 28:6–9; 36:3), his reconciliation with Jacob (see Gen. 33:1–11), and God's blessing on Ishmael and his descendants (see Gen. 17:20; 21:17–20)—the text undercuts any easy "God hates Ishmael/Esau" slogan. The story is far more nuanced—and far more hopeful. You don't need to remember every name here; the point is simpler: Scripture itself complicates the slogans.

That is why The Book of Acts' outsider label matters for the text preserves a public name—*Nazōraioi*—for the whole movement. That label doesn't mean the story belonged only to traveling apostles; it also names the Jerusalem-rooted community that held continuity through Jesus' family and the elders. Acts never forces us to choose between "the Twelve" and "the family." It presents two concentric circles within one Jerusalem-rooted movement. The Twelve function as commissioned public witnesses—men sent outward, often mobile, bearing testimony under pressure.

But the continuity of the story—the remembered teaching, the adjudication of disputes, the patient guarding of covenant meaning—remains centered in Jerusalem, where Jesus' mother, brothers, and the elders hold the hearth. In other words, the early movement is not best imagined as a traveling apostolic franchise that later "adds" a Jerusalem chapter. It is a Jerusalem hearth that sends witnesses—and receives them back—so the message remains tethered to Israel's covenant story rather than drifting into conquest, speculation, or abstraction.

Seen from the vantage point of the Netzarim/Notzrim, this matters. The same Branch who fulfills Israel's hope is also the One through whom God heals estranged branches of Abraham's family. The earliest Gospel movement was not a project of conquest, but a work of reconciliation: gathering the scattered, healing the wounded, restoring the forgotten.

So, when Christians and Jews together "gang up" on Muslims, we repeat the same amnesia that once distanced the church from Israel. Recovering the identity of the Netzarim/ Notzrim restores this truth: the family God blesses is larger than the lines we draw.

Why This Matters Now

In an age when Jewish-Christian and Muslim-Christian relations are strained by fear, trauma, and misunderstanding, recovering the meaning of Netzarim/Notzrim helps us step into the story with clarity and humility. It reminds Christians that the first followers of Jesus belonged inside Israel's covenantal world; that the nations were always meant to be included through Israel's mercy; and that the children of Ishmael and the line of Esau are not theological junk to be discarded, but part of the family horizon God promised Abraham.

This small word, often misused or misunderstood, becomes a doorway to better conversations, deeper healing, restored memory, and renewed hope. It reminds us that the story begins not in Rome, not in councils or creeds, but in the hills of Galilee—in the faith of a Jewish mother, in the courage of two Jewish brothers, in a remnant community still known as the Netzarim/Notzrim.

Chapter 9—Remembering the Abrahamic Families Today

"For I know him, (Ishmael) that he will command his children and his household after him . . . to do justice and judgment."

—Genesis 18:19

"Thou shalt not abhor an Edomite; for he is thy brother"

—Deuteronomy 23:7 (KJV)

To enter the world of Jesus' family is to step into the older, wider household of Abraham—Israel and Judah, Edom and Ishmael, Samaria and Galilee, Judeans and Arabs, synagogue and church, and the tangled afterlives of all those names in late antiquity and in our own headlines. This is why the question of "memory" in the Holy Land is never neutral: it touches Jewish self-understanding, Qur'anic reverberations, Christian identity, and the often-invisible suffering and faithfulness of Arab believers who live close to the places Western Christians fly over, photograph, and then explain back to them.

If the Gospel is truly about reconciliation, then we cannot keep listening only to the winners, the empires, or the loudest claimants to the land; we must also listen—humbly—to Middle Eastern testimonies about Jesus that survived in the cracks: in marginalized communities, contested languages, guarded traditions, and families who carried stories not as ideas, but as inheritance. Even some Western historians—James D. Tabor among them—have urged a return to the Hebraic world of Jesus. But the following is asking for more than a reset of ideas. It is a reset of listening so that the memories of Jesus carried in the Middle East are not treated as footnotes to Rome.

Beyond the "Great Tradition" of the West

To get even a glimpse of them, we must do something uncomfortable for Western Christians: we must listen, humbly, to memories of Jesus that did not pass only through the later Mediterranean Church. Our default instinct is to go West—Rome, Augustine, councils, creeds. Yet if we want to speak responsibly about "Rome," we also must resist turning the conversation into a personality cult—one pope, one news cycle, one set of hot takes. As Leonardo De Chirico argues in his Protestant reading of Pope Francis's papacy, the question is not whether Francis was a strange exception, but how he functioned as a thoroughly Roman Catholic pope—coherent within a larger post–Vatican II system and trajectory. From an evangelical vantage point, De Chirico's sustained project offers careful, historically alert assessments rather than headline-driven reactions.[1]

Yet evangelicalism is hardly immune to the same temptation. We can slip into our own "Rome" patterns—less in stone basilicas, more in celebrity platforms: the gravitational pull of a gifted preacher, a brand, a conference circuit, a podcast empire. At our best, we receive teachers as servants. At our worst, personalities become centers of meaning and the Gospel quietly gets filtered through charisma, influence networks, and the logic of scale. In other words: we may not build basilicas, but we build followings. And when the platform becomes the altar, discernment becomes disloyalty, accountability becomes attack, and truth gets measured by reach.

This is why discernment matters—and why the "Rome" question needs to be handled with both honesty and restraint. Rome has undeniably absorbed, renamed, and often re-centered many Hebraisms. Yet that absorption is not always simple theft; it can also function as a kind of depository, preserving fragments it did not originate. The question Vatican II leaves hanging is whether Rome has truly been displaced from the center—or whether the center has simply been reframed, with the same gravitational pull under new vocabulary. Evangelicalism may face a parallel predicament: we can reject one center while quietly rebuilding another.

1. De Chirico, *Fully Roman Catholic*.

A small, stubborn Jewish memory helps me keep my balance. In the rabbinic tradition about Jacob's burial, Esau contests the right to the Cave of Machpelah—seeking a claim on the fathers even while standing outside Jacob's covenant line. Later retellings sharpen the irony with a strange, unsettling image: Esau's head ends up inside the cave while his body remains outside. The picture is almost unbearable in its clarity—an embodied parable of Edom: proximity without submission, inheritance claimed without the wound of repentance, a desire to belong to the fathers while resisting the covenant that makes the fathers "fathers" in the first place.[2] Some later interpretive glosses press the symbolism even further: Esau's "head"—intellect, formation, even the residue of being taught Torah by Isaac—can be honored, while his "body"—the weight of an unyoked life, lived in the world's terms—cannot. Whether one accepts that explanation or not, the midrashic nerve is easy to feel Edom wants the fathers without the yoke of the fathers—inheritance without covenantal submission.

That nerve is exactly what Jewish memory tends to hear whenever a Christian center—Roman or evangelical—claims Israel's treasures while quietly recentering them around another throne. It is one thing to confess Israel's Messiah. It is another to take Israel's Scriptures, Israel's symbols, and Israel's promises, and then treat Israel herself as a dispensable wrapper once the "real meaning" has been extracted. In that move, the cave becomes a metaphor: the fathers are honored in name, but the covenant that formed them is resisted in practice.

I saw a recent version of this "center of gravity" tension up close at the fourth Lausanne Congress. In her plenary on justice ("Walking Humbly with God," framed by Micah 6:8), Ruth Padilla DeBorst briefly named the suffering in Gaza and warned against "colonialist theologies" that can justify oppression "under the guise of . . . dispensational eschatology."[3] The response was immediate and mixed. Some delegates heard a necessary prophetic clarity; others experienced the remarks as unbalanced—especially those shaped by dispensational streams and those engaged in Jewish/Israel-related ministries. Congress leadership soon issued an apology email acknowledging the pain caused and noting that the wording had not been adequately reviewed beforehand.

2. b. Sotah 13a (Steinsaltz) (Jacob's burial; the Machpelah dispute; Hushim son of Dan in many tellings).

3. Padilla DeBorst, "Walking Humbly with God."

If there was a "compromise," it wasn't a neat resolution so much as an institutional attempt to hold a global room together: an apology that tried to honor offended constituencies while still leaving space for reconciliation-oriented testimony—including a later plenary moment that included a Palestinian Christian voice speaking from inside the conflict. The point for my argument is not to score a political win. It is to name how easily any movement—Rome or evangelical—can feel the gravitational pull of its own donor bases, reflexes, and "approved" vocabularies.

And it's worth noticing that some of those same overlapping evangelical constituencies exist well beyond Lausanne. But the following is encouraging. In 2025, the World Evangelical Alliance installed Rev. Adv. Botrus Mansour as its Secretary General and CEO—an Arab Christian from Nazareth, described by WEA as "a Palestinian Christian from Israel," and also connected to Lausanne's reconciliation work in Israel-Palestine. Whatever one thinks about evangelical institutions, that is at least a sign that the wider evangelical world is being pressed—slowly, imperfectly—toward a fuller awareness that the Body of Christ includes long-suffering Arab and Palestinian believers too.[4]

And if the point is listening, then we should also hear voices from Bethlehem that are pleading with Western Christians not only to reject replacement theology but to refuse a different kind of displacement: the quiet swapping of the crucified Messiah for political loyalty. In an essay dated November 13, 2025, Rev. Dr. Jack Sara—of Bethlehem Bible College and a leader within the Jerusalem Alliance Church—argues that the most dangerous "replacement theology" now spreading in Western pulpits is not "the Church replacing Israel," but Israel (as a state) replacing Jesus: the flag rising above the cross, prophecy language becoming a shield for moral exemption, and Holy Land itineraries curated to see stones while bypassing the living Arab church.[5]

Whether one agrees with every line of his plea or not, his warning lands squarely on the "center of gravity" question: whenever any movement makes its identity untouchable—Rome, a nation-state, or an evangelical platform—the Gospel is no longer governing the center; the center is governing the Gospel.

4. World Evangelical Alliance's installation of Rev. Adv. Botrus Mansour—described by WEA as "a Palestinian Christian from Israel"—as Secretary General, October 31, 2025.

5. Sara, "Replacement Theology Is a Heresy."

The Family That Guarded the Evangelion

Those early communities did not always argue in the language of later theology. They did not leave us systematic dogmatics. But they did preserve memories we have largely forgotten:

- Jesus remembered as a consecrated Jew, for whom vows and embodied faithfulness mattered.
- Table remembered as covenant—not merely ritual or boundary-marker.
- A ministry shaped in Galilee and Judea's borderlands, not in imperial capitals.
- A family—Mary, James, Jude, and kin—guarding the movement's shape before anyone had heard of a bishop in Rome.

It may well have been precisely these kinds of communities—rooted in Jerusalem, allied to the family of Jesus, and spread through synagogues and households of the East—who gathered, copied, and preserved the writings we now call the New Testament. After James' martyrdom, ancient tradition remembers Symeon (Simon) son of Clopas—a relative of Jesus—as the one who stepped into leadership in Jerusalem.[6]

It's not hard to imagine that under James—and then Symeon—through the years leading up to the Temple's destruction and into the long, painful road toward Yavneh (the period Christians often speak of, a bit too quickly, as the "beginning of Rabbinic Judaism"), these family-linked assemblies were among those who cherished, ordered, and handed on what they simply called the Evangelion: the Gospel in its fullness.

To speak this way about the Netzarim/Notzrim is not to carve out a small "saved Israel" over against a "rejected Israel." It is to name a vocation inside Israel's own life. Jews who followed Yeshua did not stop belonging to their people; they became one strand of Israel's covenantal faithfulness—a strand that opened a lawful path for the nations—without cancelling the other strands God was still weaving.

If later Christian and even Messianic language turned "Jews who accepted Jesus" into the real Israel and everyone else into castaways, that is exactly the kind of internal "replacement theology" this book is trying to refuse. Romans 11 will not let us shrink Israel down to one party in the story; it insists on a mystery in which "all Israel" still stands under

6. Eusebius, *Ecclesiastical History* 3.11.1–2.

promise, even as one stream within Israel carries a particular calling for the sake of the nations.

Paul and James: Halakhah for the Nations

It is no accident that the New Testament as we have it is mostly Pauline. The same family-led communities that guarded the Evangelion also recognized that the nations needed a clear halakhic path. Paul had been trained "at the feet of Gamaliel" (Acts 22:3), a Pharisee of the Hillelite stream (see Acts 5:34) who defended the early disciples. Paul was not some freelance innovator; he carried into the Gentile mission the tools of a Pharisee formed in the tradition that shaped James and the Jerusalem assembly.

Jesus Himself had already affirmed this Pharisaic authority in Matthew 23 when He said, "The scribes and the Pharisees sit in Moses' seat. So do and observe whatever they tell you, but not the works they do." That word is first about their Judaism—their halakhic teaching for Israel—because the "seat of Moses" was the bema of the synagogue, the place from which both Jews and God-fearing Gentiles were instructed.

Gentiles were never being told to "do what they do" in the sense of taking on Israel's full yoke, but to hear and respond to the Noahide—or "Way"—teaching that flowed from that same seat. We often miss this because we collapse the whole chapter into the later rebukes, as if Jesus were cancelling all Pharisaic authority, instead of exposing the same kind of showy religious hypocrisy we still see today—people who honor God with their lips and their Sundays but live like the devil the rest of the week.

For modern Christians, this question of boundary-marking is not abstract. It sits right on the fault line of one of our biggest theological debates today (as I noted in Interlude 1): the divide between the Reformed tradition and the New Perspective on Paul. The Reformed world hears Paul warning against self-salvation through moral effort; the New Perspective hears Paul confronting the use of Jewish identity markers that kept Gentiles at arm's length. Both hear something real. And scholars like Mark Nanos have helped clarify that Paul's phrase "works of the law" often lands precisely on boundary-marking practices—the social lines that defined who was inside and outside the covenant community, especially in an empire where Judaism enjoyed a measure of legal toleration and negotiated protections, while new, undefined movements could be treated as suspect. Religious nominalism is not new.

The Crux of the Cross

But if we want to hear Paul with Middle Eastern ears, we must add one more layer—one that Imperial Rome understood instinctively. The Torah says, "*Cursed is everyone who hangs on a tree*" (Deut. 21:23), and the Roman state perfected a way of putting people on trees in public. Crucifixion was not merely execution; it was weaponized shame—a terror-technology meant to keep Judeans (and every subject people) in check: "This is what happens when you resist." In that world, "cursed" was not only a religious category; it became a political one. Rome could make a man look abandoned by God and crushed by Caesar in the same spectacle.

That is why Paul's claim in Galatians hits like a thunderclap: the Messiah became that "curse" for us—not because Torah was wrong, but because Torah named the horror honestly—so that the blessing promised to Abraham could reach the nations (see Gal. 3:13–14). Paul was not abolishing Torah, nor was he lowering the bar for Gentiles. He was guarding the covenant from being turned into a fence, and he was also announcing that Rome's favorite tool of intimidation had been turned inside out. The cross was meant to seal the boundary with fear; Paul proclaims it as the place where God breaks the curse-logic, exposes the empire's violence, and opens the family of Abraham to those who were never supposed to get in.

A Table-Shaped Gospel

Seen through the eyes of Jesus' family, Paul's letters look far less like a break with Judaism and far more like a halakhic defense of table fellowship—protecting Israel's calling and protecting the nations from being forced into an identity never meant for them. And if Paul sounds like the family's defense attorney for the nations, James sounds like the householder writing down the house rules.

In his little book, James assumes a community that still calls its gathering a synagōgē—an assembly that must decide who sits where and on what terms. He warns them not to give the man with the gold ring and fine clothing the best seat while telling the poor man, "Stand there" or "Sit at my feet." He insists that "faith without works is dead," not as a denial of grace, but as a defense of a table where the hungry brother or sister must not be sent away with pious words and an empty stomach. He defines "pure and undefiled religion" as visiting orphans and widows in their affliction and keeping oneself unstained by the world. In other words, James is not writing abstract doctrine; he is spelling out what a table-shaped community looks like when the Lord of glory walks into the room and sits the poor in places of honor.

When the first great table crisis hit—the clash in Antioch over who could eat with whom—Paul did not appeal to his own authority alone. He pointed back to what had already been agreed in Jerusalem, under James' leadership: that Gentiles were to turn from idols, blood, strangled meat, and sexual immorality, and so share the table without becoming Jews (see Acts 15). James becomes, in that sense, the first halakhic voice of the table for the nations. If Jude gives us the alarm bell, James gives us the house rules.

When these communities gathered and copied their Scriptures, it makes sense that they preserved so many of Paul's letters—not because Paul displaced the family of Jesus, but because his letters translated the family's covenantal faith into the soil of the nations. The Book of Acts shows him repeatedly in conversation and cooperation with the Jerusalem leaders (see Acts 15; 21); the majority of historical Jesus scholars need to see that Paul was no enemy of Jesus' family but their partner in extending the same Gospel to the ends of the earth.

In that light, the Evangelion is not something other than the New Testament; it is what the New Testament already is: the collected witness of Jesus' family and their coworkers—James, Peter, Jude, Paul, and others—ordered in such a way that Paul's Hillelite, Gamaliel-shaped halakhic imagination could serve the nations without severing them from Israel's covenant. In that sense, the New Testament functions almost like a kind of Mishnah for the nations—an oral Torah written down, a "spoonful of sugar" that lets the medicine of Torah go down as good news rather than as a crushing burden, teaching Gentiles how to walk in Israel's story without pretending to become Israel.

People of the Table: Original Christianity

One of the voices who has helped me listen to these Middle Eastern echoes is an Orthodox Jewish historian, Ben Abrahamson, mentioned previously. After making aliyah to Israel in the 1980s during the first Intifada and experiencing the wounds of distorted Islamic inspired violence firsthand, he became determined to understand Muslims and to build bridges rather than walls. From his institute in Jerusalem, he has cultivated deep relationships with Muslim scholars, acted as a quiet advocate for peace, and produced a series of books and studies that deserve far wider publication.

His work on the *People of the Table* explores how Jewish and Jewish-Christian memories of Jesus survived outside both church comfort zones and later Rabbinic silences, taking seriously the possibility that Jesus' earliest followers were halakhic Jews whose common life revolved around a consecrated table.

At the center of that work is the Qur'an's brief but striking story of the "People of the Table" (Q 5:112–115), where Jesus' disciples ask for a table to be sent down from heaven as a sign, a festival, and a test. Read through the lens of Torah and the Mishnah, Ben argues this is not a random miracle story but a memory of the Nazarite completion meal—a halakhic table where a consecrated vow-taker shares portions of a sacrificial feast with others, including those normally kept at the margins.

A clarification matters here: there is a difference between reading the earliest Qur'anic material as a witness to the religious world of late antiquity (and to possible echoes of older Jewish and Jesus-disciple memories) and treating Islam as the fully developed classical system that later emerged under empire. The Qur'an's textual roots belong to the first/seventh-century milieu of early manuscript witness that was already circulating close to that period.

So, when this book listens to "Middle Eastern echoes," it is not granting a new authority over the apostolic witness; it is distinguishing early textual/ritual memory from later imperial codification whether Christendom or Islam—and using that distinction to illuminate how the Jesus-family stream understood covenant, table, and the nations.

In Abrahamson's view, Islam often preserves this older, covenantal layer of Jesus' mission—Jesus as a Torah-faithful vow-taker gathering Israelites and God-fearing nations around a sanctified table—long after Gentile Christianity had shifted its focus to metaphysics and sacramental theories. For my purposes in this book, the point is simple: this Middle Eastern memory highlights just how Jewish, how halakhic, and how table-centered our own New Testament already is.

I felt the weight of that not first in a library, but in our little congregation in Rome. On paper, we were simply "celebrating the Lord's Supper." The room was full of people who carried complicated stories— immigrant women living with Italian men they were not married to, men who felt disqualified by their past, immigrants who had been told in other churches that they were not "ready" for the table. Some were not even formal members, Roman Catholics who just assumed the Eucharist at a church service, but they were hungry.

I could hear, in the back of my mind, the same accusations that were thrown at Jesus: "*This man receives sinners and eats with them*" (Luke 15:2). He did not deny it. He answered with a story about a lost sheep, a lost coin, a lost son, and with a table where the father says, "*It was fitting to celebrate and be glad*" (Luke 15:32). He had already said, "*It is not the healthy who need a physician, but those who are sick. I have not come to call the righteous but sinners*" (Luke 5:31–32, NASB). At another meal, He allowed a woman known as a sinner to wash His feet with her tears and told her, "*Your faith has saved you; go in peace*" (Luke 7:50).

And alongside those memories I could hear James whispering his questions to my own heart: "*My brothers, show no partiality as you hold the faith in our Lord Jesus Christ, the Lord of glory*" (James 2:1). If a richly dressed person is welcomed with honor while the poor one is told to stand in the back, "*Have you not then made distinctions among yourselves and become judges with evil thoughts?*" (James 2:4). A table that forgets the poor, James says, has forgotten its Lord.

I could not turn the table into a reward for people who already felt sorted out. So, even when some could not in good conscience join in the bread and the cup, I made it a point to pray over everyone in the room—to name the Lord's Supper as a place where the unworthy are sought, where sinners are invited to know Him in the breaking of the bread, and where those on the margins can begin to believe that this meal is also for them. If Jesus' first critics were scandalized that He "*ate with tax collectors and sinners*," then it should not surprise us that our own tables will be haunted by the same question: Who is allowed to sit here and on what terms?

From Havdalah to the Lord's Supper

From that vantage point, several New Testament details that we usually skim suddenly matter. Already in Acts we find the disciples "breaking bread" on a Saturday night (see Acts 20) after the Sabbath day was over. For Jews, that time is not an afterthought; it is charged with meaning. The transition from Sabbath into the week is marked by *havdalah*—a ceremony that blesses the One who separates holy from ordinary—and in many communities, by *melaveh malchah*, "accompanying the King" or the Queen of Shabbat out into the workweek.[7]

Seen in that light, the Lord's Supper is not a strange ritual dropped into history. It is a Jewish rhythm: after Sabbath rest, the community gathers around bread and cup and re-enters the week as witnesses. So, when Paul reminds the 1 Corinthians 11 that "*on the night he was betrayed*" Jesus took bread, broke it, and said, "*Do this in remembrance of me*," he is not inventing a clerical sacrament to be managed from above. He is taking an existing table-rhythm and filling it with Passover meaning (see 1 Cor. 5:7)—telling Israel's story to Gentiles through a shared meal. For Paul, the table becomes the place the community re-confesses its faith week by week, moving from Sabbath light into the calling of the nations. This was the first thing I learned from Yossi as he tried to re-center his listeners on the table during the COVID shutdown.

In that world, a "table of the Lord" is not an abstract doctrine. It is where marginal Israelites and God-fearing outsiders are brought in lawfully; where the poor and the infirm are seen and seated; where vows, purity, and mercy meet around bread and wine; and where the rested community re-commits itself to go out as His witnesses. From the Middle Eastern side, then, Jesus is not remembered as one who broke Torah to show grace, but as one who used Torah's own structures—vows, boundary-markers, and havdalah-like transitions—to gather the wounded edges of Israel and open a lawful path for the nations.

Three Streams and the Fight for the Evangelion

Abrahamson also proposes that, in those early centuries, Jewish memory could still distinguish three streams within the Jesus movement:

1. A Nazarene/Nazarite stream, centered on consecration, Temple piety, and Jesus' own family.
2. A Tobiad/Notzri stream that, in some expressions, drifted toward mixed and speculative ideas—sometimes shading into proto-Gnostic patterns.
3. A Hellenized God-fearer stream that grew rapidly among the nations, often at a distance from Jewish halakhah.

7. Mishnah Berakhot 8:5; Shulchan Arukh, Orach Chayim 296:1 (havdalah); b. Shabbat 119b; Shulchan Arukh, Orach Chayim 300:1 (melaveh malkah).

You do not have to master the terminology. The point is simple: vocation and distortion travel side by side. If it helps, think of it—very roughly—like the difference between the Sadducean stream of Temple-aristocratic power nominalism and the Pharisaic stream of covenant practice and resurrection hope faithfulness that provided hope.

In the first century, the sharpest line did not finally run between "Yeshua-Jews" and "other Jews," but between those who clung to the hope of resurrection in the age to come and covenant mercy and those who flattened that hope into status, power, or despair as a form of religion in name only not the relationship with the One who reveals. The family-led Nazarene stream is, in my reading, one way Israel's own hope for resurrection and renewal took shape—a calling within Israel, not a replacement of Israel.

Jude's little letter sits inside a world where rival stories about Jesus were already circulating and where the family stream—with James as the recognizable head of the Jerusalem assembly and Jude sounding the warning from the edges—was fighting to keep the Evangelion whole. That is exactly the world this book has been trying to recover: not a Jesus floating above Judaism, but a Jesus whose family guarded a Jewish, covenantal, consecrated way of following Him—and whose communities, under pressure, preserved and handed on the Evangelion that became our New Testament. Middle Eastern memories don't replace our Gospels or create a new authority tier. They function more like light from the side, illuminating the texture of the world James and Jude took for granted.

To enter these memories is also to feel the ache of boundary-making. After AD 70, synagogue life had to be rebuilt, and in that rebuilding, Jewish leaders increasingly clarified what belonged "inside" and what did not. Later Jewish tradition preserves this sharpening in the Birkat ha-Minim—a liturgical benediction directed against "sectarians." In a world where communities were reforming identity under pressure, Jesus-confessing Jews were increasingly forced to decide whether their confession could remain one voice within Israel or whether it would be pushed out into a separate social world. Human nature shows itself here: boundary-making can become a form of protection, but it can also harden into reflex, and the scars of that hardening are still visible in our own day. That pressure is one reason "memory" in the Holy Land is never neutral: it is carried not only in texts, but in communities learning how to survive.

And not all "Middle Eastern memory" is rabbinic. Eastern Christian memory also survived outside the Latin West, namely the Oriental Orthodox—in Syriac-speaking communities, in the ancient Coptic and

Armenian traditions, and in severe forms of embodied witness like the stylites who sat in their high towers, whose lives became public sermons of repentance, prayer, and endurance.

These churches did not generate the kind of expansionist, coercive "Christian empire" that later marked parts of the Latin West; more often they endured as vulnerable communities—close to the Holy Land in language, liturgy, and habitus—under larger powers and shifting regimes. Many of them belong to the non-Chalcedonian churches.[8]

In the New Testament, the Jews remain the oracle-keepers: those to whom, Paul says, "*were entrusted with the oracles of God*" (Rom. 3:2). The Gospel does not cancel that vocation; it intensifies it—because the nations are brought into Israel's covenant drama rather than extracted into a rival one (see Rom. 11). The nations are invited in, but they are not handed a different God or a different story; they are summoned to love the God of Israel, receive the Messiah of Israel, and honor the Scriptures that first named Him.

And what about Jewish voices today—after the long centuries of pressure, polemic, and survival? They are still there hanging out by a thread: arguing with the text, praying the text, guarding the text, and refusing to let the Name be domesticated by empire even that of the State of Israel.[9] For the nations, that ongoing Jewish witness is not an obstacle to the Gospel; it is part of the world the Gospel addresses. Listening does not mean surrendering confession. It means remembering that Gentiles were invited in as guests and grafted branches—never as owners.

And the reach of that living Jewish memory has never been confined to synagogue walls. Even the "secular" soundtracks many of us grew up on—protest songs, rock lyrics, the poetry of cultural dissent—have often

8. "Oriental Orthodox" is now the generally accepted umbrella term for these non-Chalcedonian churches, which is they have a different view on Christology and perhaps more in line with Yeshua Sar Haphanim as presented in chapter 6.

9. Chardal names a rigorist Religious-Zionist current that has, in some settings, assumed the mantle of "Orthodox"—itself a modern label—functioning as one expression within the contested Zionist phenomenon. By contrast, the Edah HaChareidis denotes a Jerusalem Charedi communal body identified with strong anti-Zionism and in many cases, non-recognition of the state, presenting itself as continuity with pre-modern Judaism and with the long Jewish pattern of sustaining Torah life across many nations and empires. At the same time, whatever one's theological reading of Zionism, the modern State of Israel has undeniably provided a physical haven in which Charedi Torah study and communal life could rebuild and flourish after the catastrophes of modern Europe—yet in recent years, that space has also felt newly fragile and contested, increasingly subject to internal political pressures, including intensified disputes over military conscription and the long-standing exemptions granted to many Charedim.

been carried by Jewish voices, sometimes naming nothing overtly "religious," yet still drawing from a deep inheritance: exile and longing, justice and lament, hope without naïveté, and a stubborn refusal to let empire have the last word. Collective memory is a reality. It travels—through prayer and commentary, yes, but also through art, music, and public speech. And if we can recognize that in the cultural register, we should not be surprised to find it in the covenantal one.

Why Does That Matter for a Book About the "Last Days"?

Because if these older Jewish memories are even partly right, then the ground shifts beneath so much modern end-times talk:

- The earliest Jesus movement was born around a table of consecration, not a countdown of terrors.
- The first "last days" were not about escape from the world, but about holiness and mercy in the middle of it.
- The family of Jesus did not preach a faith that cancels Israel, but a faith that heals Israel's wounds and opens the gate for Edom, Ishmael, and the nations.

In other words, the "forgotten Middle Eastern Jesus" looks a lot like the one His mother and His brothers—James and Jude—and His cousins actually knew and like the Jesus the Twelve carried to the ends of the earth: not a mascot for panic, but Israel's Messiah forming a people.

And that brings me back to something that has been quietly accompanying me since childhood: a strange little German fable about four unwanted animals on their way to Bremen—an image I'll use in the epilogue as a parable of the people of God.

Bremen is not only a storybook place for me. It is where the Doulos ship was refitted in the late 1970s for more than 30 years of ministry—and where my shipmates and I visited during Christmas 1984. I am unapologetically a disciple and an evangelist. This is the "homework" I have done so that I may witness better; but when I look back, what I most clearly see is His Presence. The ship itself now lives on as a hotel/museum in Southeast Asia.[10] May we learn to walk in His Presence and in the best sense of Simpson's old phrase, "bring back the King."

10. https://www.cnn.com/2025/08/20/style/indonesia-doulos-phos-ship-hotel-hnk-intl-dst

Epilogue—When the Family Gathers Again

"For the earth shall be filled with the knowledge of the glory of the LORD, as the waters cover the sea."

—HABAKKUK 2:14

LONG BEFORE I HAD language for "Kingdom now and not yet," that verse was already in my bones. On OM's ships it became the closing song of our international nights—a simple chorus from Habakkuk, sung in many accents and tongues as we stood shoulder to shoulder in national dress. Life on board sometimes felt like a rehearsal for the day when "*the earth will be filled with the knowledge of the LORD.*" It gave us a kind of shared joy—a community experience—and friendships we still treasure after many years.

In our small, fragile way, we were already tasting that future: an international fellowship worshiping together, witnessing among the nations, stumbling toward holiness, learning to love and serve one another. I didn't have the words then, but it was a "Kingdom now" moment—imperfect, unfinished, and yet undeniably real.

Fear usually loosens its grip in a quiet way—rarely dramatic, often unnoticed. For me, that shift came when I stopped feeding on the noise of the prophecy industry—charts, countdowns, and manufactured urgency—and began listening again to truer voices: the steady witness of former shipmates, and then more recently, the voices that were there from the beginning—not only the songs we sang at sea, but the family who first lived this story.

The Twelve were never meant to replace the family, and the family was never meant to shrink the mission; the healed future gathers both—witness and continuity—into one reconciled household. In Israel's own vocabulary, you might say it like this: the movement needed both qahal and edah. The qahal gathers, listens, remembers—guarding covenant posture so that zeal does not outrun obedience. The edah goes out, bears witness, risks misunderstanding—carrying testimony into public life as a visible sign. Jerusalem and the family kept the hearth.

The Twelve carried the witness. When those callings remained in relationship, the movement stayed sane: humility before urgency, listening before sending, mercy before spectacle. The tragedy of later history is that these were torn apart—mission without trembling on the one side and guarding without outward witness on the other. But the healed future gathers them again.

Mary. James. Jude. The ones who carried the story before anyone tried to turn it into a system. They were never panicked. They were never decoding Rome. They were never looking for escape. They held the story differently—anciently, as covenant, faithfully. And when I returned to them, something in me opened. The fear began to crack. Because the Last Days were never about evacuation. They were always about restoration.

The Messiah at Rome's Gates

There is a Jewish story that says this with a clarity I never learned from prophecy charts. A rabbi asks Elijah when the Messianic redemption will manifest. Elijah replies that the Messiah is already here sitting at the gates of Rome among the afflicted. The rabbi goes and finds Him outside the city, where empire leaves its wounded. One detail grabs him: the sick unwrap their bandages all at once and then wrap them again, but the Messiah binds His wounds one at a time—always ready to rise. The rabbi asks, "When will you come?" The Messiah answers, "Today." When the day ends without spectacle, Elijah explains the riddle with a verse: "Today—if you hear His voice."

Redemption is near, but it is not triggered by panic or conquest. It begins with recognition—with a people who stop hardening their hearts and learn how to hear again. The Messiah is not enthroned inside Rome's imagination. He sits at Rome's gate: a contradiction to empire and a sign that the Last Days are not about evacuation, but restoration.[1] I can never forget the first Keith Green song I heard—"The Sheep and the Goats" (see Matt. 25). I heard it only months before he was taken, and it tuned me to

1. b. Sanhedrin 98a; cf. Ps. 95:7–8

God's priorities: mercy at the margins and readiness to rise and go with a passion to reach the world.

The Last Days Begin When Fear Ends

Jesus never told His followers to run from the world. He told them to endure it without becoming it. To forgive when retaliation feels righteous. To bless when the moment demands a curse. To love enemies, not because enemies are harmless, but because the Father is faithful. He trained His disciples to stay awake—not in panic, not in timelines, not in the narcotic of speculation—but in compassion, clarity, and courage.

James taught a faith that works in the real world: the faith that shows up at the door, that keeps promises, that restrains the tongue, that refuses favoritism, that puts bread in a hungry hand. Jude taught a courage that contends with mercy: a courage that can name deception without losing tenderness, that can warn without turning cruel, that can fight for the faith without becoming a fighter. And Mary sang a revolution rooted in God's compassion for the lowly: not the revolution of the sword, but the overturning that begins when God lifts the humble, fills the hungry, and scatters the proud in the imagination of their hearts.

Together they form the witness we most need today. The Last Days are not an escape plan. They are not a permission slip for fear. They are not an excuse to stop loving neighbors because history is tense. They are a summons—first to fidelity, then to endurance, then to joy.

- A summons to trust that the Father's face truly shines through the Son.
- A summons to live as if mercy is more real than outrage.
- A summons to become the kind of people whose lives make God's promises look believable because they are already drawing near.

The Remnant Has Always Been Small—and Always Real

Every generation produces its own noise—religious ideologies, political constructions, fresh slogans, fresh threats. Each age crowns new prophets of certainty and appoints new merchants of dread. But the edah—the faithful witnessing remnant—has always been small. Not because God is weak, but because fidelity is never fashionable.

The remnant did not usually sit in palaces. It did not build its identity on fear. It did not need a manifesto to justify its bitterness. It carried a flame—often quietly, often painfully, often without applause. From the early Netzarim/Notzrim in Jerusalem, praying and breaking bread under pressure, to the scattered Jewish believers receiving Jude's urgent letter and learning to contend without losing mercy, to refugees and exiles, desert fathers and hidden saints, missionaries and laborers, migrants and overlooked disciples whose only eschatology was faithfulness—these were the ones who kept the story alive. Not by escaping history, but by refusing to let history rename God. And the invitation remains unchanged:

- Join the remnant who remembers mercy.
- Join the people who stay awake in love.
- Join the witnesses who endure without drifting—fixed to the Living One, until the Morning Star rises.

The Song of the Redeemed

As a child, I loved the old fables—especially *The Bremen Town Musicians*. I had no idea that story was quietly catechizing me. Only in recent years, through study, prayer, and a conversation with Yossi after October 7, 2023—did I realize I had never really interpreted it. What if *The Bremen Town Musicians* is a mashal—a parable of the restored assembly?

In our Scriptures, a mashal is more than a nice illustration. It is a story placed alongside reality so that the truth can be seen from a slant. Proverbs are mashalim and so are the parables of Jesus. A mashal does not explain everything; it opens a window. When I call *The Bremen Town Musicians* a mashal, I am not turning it into a rigid allegory but recognizing that this little German fable has been, for me, a Kingdom parable in disguise—a story about a wounded, rejected fellowship becoming an edah, a band of testimony.

And over time, the four animals have begun to look less "German" and more like the fellowships of the Middle East and beyond into free churches that were persecuted by the institutional church:

- The donkey who is redeemed—burdened but blessed: the petter ḥamor, the firstborn beast of Exodus that must be redeemed so the house can go free—Israel's remnant underweight and the humble mount Messiah chose to ride.
- The dog who is grafted in—once outside, now at the table: kelev (like Caleb)—not the kiruv snarling "dogs" of the streets Paul mentions, but the housedog, beloved and trained; the nations welcomed into Israel's household, learning to guard a story that was not originally theirs. Like the women Jesus met, who had greater faith than the lost Jews he came for.
- The cat who slips past empire—watcher in the ruins: Egypt's old creature of omen turned into a quiet survivor—nimble, half-unseen. Like the forgotten Oriental Orthodox churches—Armenian, Coptic, Assyrian, Syriac, and Ethiopian—or Arab Christians more broadly, and even the many free-church movements across history that were persecuted by institutional Christianity: a "trail of blood," not a paper trail—rarely preserved in the annals of the victors except as "heretics." Yet they kept vigil at the edges through empires, caliphates, crusades, and controversies.
- The rooster who cries at dawn—a mercy-alarm: the steeple-bird of Protestant Europe, calling conscience awake—Reformation light breaking—yet forever shadowed by Simon Peter's denial, and therefore summoning us back to humility, repentance, and covenant love.

Together they become an edah—a band of testimony, a strange fellowship: a donkey, a dog, a cat, and a rooster, Jewish and Gentile, Eastern and Western, huddled together in a house that used to be a den of robbers, now turned, by grace, into a place of praise by their joyful noise that scarred the robbers away. In that sense, Bremen is already singing what the prophets saw from afar: former enemies gathered under one roof, learning a new song together. Long before anyone steps onto Isaiah's highway, the animals are already sharing the house.

A Highway Between Enemies

> *"In that day there will be a highway from Egypt to Assyria, and Assyria will come into Egypt, and Egypt into Assyria, and the Egyptians will worship with the Assyrians."*
>
> —Isaiah 19:23

If Bremen gives us a house once filled with robbers turned into a place of praise, Isaiah 19 gives us the same miracle stretched out across a map. The prophets saw something we still struggle to believe: not just the survival of Israel, but a day when former enemies would share a road and a song. Egypt and Assyria—names we mostly remember as slave-masters and invaders—are suddenly pictured as fellow worshipers, walking the same highway toward the God of Israel.

That is the surprise at the heart of the Last Days. The story does not end with sealed borders and perfect tribes. It ends with a road cut through old hostilities, with Edom and Ishmael invited in, with Egyptians and Assyrians learning the liturgy of mercy alongside Jacob's children.

If Isaiah is right, then the final word over history is not "us versus them," but "blessed be Egypt my people, and Assyria the work of my hands, and Israel my inheritance" (Isa. 19:25). The highway between enemies is already under construction—in every act of repentance, every table opened, every wound offered back to the One who refuses to let the family story fracture forever. The Last Days are not the closure of that road. They are the moment we finally step onto it.

Jesus Is Still the Face of the Father

If this book has done anything, I pray it has lifted our eyes past the panic and back to the Person.

Jesus does not reveal a God in retreat. He reveals a Father who runs toward His children.

- A Father whose justice never abandons compassion.
- A Father who keeps covenant even when we forget.
- A Father who refuses to lose Israel—or the nations—or the ones who wander farthest.

When Jesus spoke of the Last Days, He was not describing a collapse of hope. He was describing the birth pangs of restoration. The shaking is real. But so is the promise.

Torat Edom and the Hope of the Wounded

This whole journey has been, in its own way, an exploration of Torat Edom—the teaching that arises from the wound, the reconciliation that begins where the fracture was deepest, the Messiah mending what exile and empire tore apart.

- From Jacob's well to the broken communities of Judea and Samaria . . .
- From Ishmael's descendants to the edges of the nations . . .
- From the scattered tribes to the wandering prodigals . . .

Jesus gathers the estranged and refuses to let the family story collapse. This is not sentiment. It is the heart of eschatology.

The Story God Refuses to End

For all the noise we inherited—the prophecy charts, the geopolitical nightmares, the attempts to calculate the end—the New Testament closes with something far quieter and far more human:

"*The Spirit and the Bride say, 'Come'*" (Rev. 22:17).

- A family calling its members home.
- A world thirsting for living water.
- A Messiah still gathering His people from every direction.

And this is where the qahal and the edah finally meet without rivalry. The Bride is a gathered people—formed by listening, by memory, by covenant mercy. Yet the same Bride is also a witnessing people—sent into the world with lamp and oil, bread and water, courage and consolation. The Last Days, in that light, are not an escape plan but a posture: a people who listen before speaking, who remember before innovating, who walk humbly before being sent, and who bear witness without forgetting where we came from—until the City descends and the family is whole.

Perhaps this is what Mary, James, and Jude understood all along: The Last Days are not the end of the world. They are the end of forgetting who we are. A people shaped by promise. A family mended by mercy. A story held open by the One who still says—in every generation, every tongue, every shadow, every dawn:

Do not be afraid.

I am with you.

Come home.

Appendix 1—The Last Days According to the Bible

> *"In the past God spoke to our ancestors through the prophets at many times and in various ways, but in these last days he has spoken to us by his Son"*
>
> —HEBREWS 1:1–2 (NIV)

WHEN MOST PEOPLE HEAR "the last days," or eschatology (the systematic study of the subject), they often picture countdown clocks, secret plots, and a tiny remnant hiding somewhere with canned goods. The Bible's own way of speaking is very different. "Last days" is not a brand for Christian panic. It is the way Scripture talks about God bringing His covenant story with Israel and the nations to its fullness.

Those two time-phrases from the book of Hebrews—"long ago" and "in these last days"—are like two bookends on the covenant story. But it is important to notice something else about Hebrews. Despite its title in our Bibles, it is not a tract against "the Jews," nor is it a private memo to one ethnic group. It is a proclamation that the God of Israel, who spoke to "the fathers" by the prophets, is now speaking to us—Jews and nations together—through the Son.

Here a distinction helps: all Jews are Hebrews, but not all Hebrews are Jews. "Hebrew" is the older, wider family-name that reaches back to Abraham and, I would argue, even to the sons of God in the pre-Noahic age when the Hebrew calendar began. It can stretch outward to include those from the nations who come to share Abraham's faith. In that sense, Hebrews is not a book written away from the Jews; it is written out from within Israel's story to invite the world into that Hebraic faithfulness. It calls us in the nations to become "Hebrews" in this older sense—people who cross over from idolatry to the living God, who attach ourselves to Israel's Messiah and to the God who raised Him from the dead. With that in mind, we can hear "the last days" in its proper key.

Long before the New Testament, Israel's prophets were already speaking of "the latter days" or "the end of days." In Deuteronomy, Moses warns that Israel will disobey, be scattered, and then return to the Lord "in the latter days"—judgment, yes, but also mercy and return (see Deut. 4:29–31; 31:29). Isaiah and Micah picture a time when the mountain of the Lord is lifted up, Torah goes out from Zion, and the nations stream in to learn His ways. Swords become plowshares; peoples "learn war no more" (see Isa. 2:2–4; Mic. 4:1–4). Other prophets speak of a shaken Israel, a preserved remnant, and nations turning toward the God of Jacob (see Isa. 11; Amos 9:11–12; Zech. 8:20–23).

From the beginning, then, "last days" language is covenantal: it is about God keeping His promises to Abraham, Isaac, and Jacob—and through them to all the families of the earth.

The New Testament does not introduce the phrase; it announces that those days have already begun. Hebrews says God has spoken "in these last days" by His Son (see Heb. 1:1–2). Peter explains Pentecost by quoting Joel and saying, "*This is what was uttered . . . 'In the last days . . . I will pour out my Spirit on all flesh*'" (Acts 2:16–17). Paul can say that "*the end of the ages has come*" (1 Cor. 10:11).

For the first followers of Jesus, the Last Days are not a future movie; they are the time opened by Messiah's death, Resurrection, and exaltation. The old age of sin and death is still grinding on, but the age to come has already broken in. We live in the overlap. Within that overlap, certain things are meant to ripen. Israel's story is not discarded; it is intensified. There is real judgment on unfaithful leadership and on the Temple system Jesus wept over (see Matt. 23–24), yet there remains a mysterious, ongoing election of Israel that Paul refuses to cancel (see Rom. 11:1–2, 28–29). The stumbling of Israel becomes the doorway for mercy to the nations, and mercy to the nations is meant to provoke Israel to jealousy, not contempt (see Rom. 11:11–15, 25–32).

At the same time, the nations are being grafted in. Gentiles are not a new tree; they are wild branches joined to Israel's cultivated olive (see Rom. 11:17–24). The Gospel is preached "*to all nations*" (Matt. 24:14), not as trivia for charts but as an invitation into covenant faithfulness. The Last Days are a time when God is forming a people marked by patient endurance, faith, and love in the midst of pressure (see 1 Thess. 1:2–3; Rev. 13:10; 14:12).

Judgment and renewal walk together here. Jesus will judge the living and the dead (see 2 Tim. 4:1), but judgment is not the final word. Creation itself will be set free from its slavery to decay (see Rom. 8:18–23). The destination is not escape from the earth but a New Heavens and a New Earth where righteousness dwells and God's dwelling is with humanity (see Isa. 65–66; 2 Pet. 3:13; Rev. 21–22).

One of the biggest distortions in our imagination has come from a single word in Revelation 20: *millennium*, repeated several times in the chapter. Through the last two millennia, this rich and mysterious chapter has been turned into a controlling paradigm. Instead of letting Revelation's "thousand years" sit inside the wider biblical story, we have allowed it to become a grid that keeps us captive inside pre-, post-, and amillennial schemes we think we must choose between—or we become frustrated and just blurt out that it will all "pan out" in the end.

In The Christian and Missionary Alliance's latest Council (June 2025), the vote was not a simple up-or-down referendum on "premillennialism." Rather, the question before us was whether to affirm the existing doctrinal language and then publish an explanatory preamble/exception to address real pastoral and practical concerns. A separate option to remove "premillennial" from the Statement of Faith was not placed on the floor as a direct vote.

Even so, the discussion revealed something important: many of us struggle to articulate what "premillennial" is meant to safeguard in practice beyond a general posture of watchfulness and missionary faithfulness (see Matt. 24:14). Our Canadian family has long taken a different path on how such language functions in a statement. The deeper issue, then, is not simply which label we retain, but whether our eschatological speech is being governed by a single apocalyptic chapter—or by the clearer, wider prophetic witness to the Messianic Age.

Meanwhile, Jewish tradition reads time through a different lens altogether: a 6,000-year pattern in which, as of the mid-2020s, we are in the late 5700s of the Hebrew calendar—not counting from a modern scientific "beginning," but from when humanity began to call upon the Name of the Lord. I am not suggesting we can be certain about any exact timeline. If anything, that uncertainty may be a gift—an invitation to hold our millennial labels more lightly, to listen again to Israel's calendar, and to recover a more biblical, less speculative way of speaking about the Last Days.

Because so much confusion and fear and division have attached themselves to this language, it helps to say plainly what the Last Days are not. They are not a license to despise Israel, Ishmael, or Esau. God's judgments are severe, but His promises and mercies toward Abraham's family and their branches run deeper than our slogans (see Gen. 17:20; Oba.; Rom. 9–11). They are not primarily about decoding geopolitics.

The New Testament spends far more energy warning about false teaching, greed, and lovelessness in the community than about international borders. Nor are they an excuse to abandon ordinary faithfulness. Paul has strong words for those who use eschatology as an alibi to stop working and drift into spiritual gossip (see 2 Thess. 3:6–13). Hope in the Lord's coming is supposed to make us steadier, not less.

Above all, the Last Days are not an alibi for fear. Again, and again the word from Jesus is, "*Do not be afraid*" (Matt. 24:6; Luke 12:32). The posture is wakefulness, not hysteria. "Stay awake," He says, and be found doing the will of the Father—caring for the least, loving one another, keeping your lamp lit.

To live in the Last Days, biblically, is to live facing Jerusalem's story honestly, rooted in Messiah's Cross and Resurrection, open to the nations we are tempted to dismiss, and shaped by faith, hope, and love (see 1 Cor. 13:13; 1 Thess, 1:3). Any end-times teaching that erodes one of those three has already drifted out of tune with Scripture.

In that sense, the Last Days are not a horror film to survive but a covenant season to inhabit: the time when the God of Abraham brings Israel's story and the story of the nations to their promised fullness in Jesus. That is the frame in which Mary sings, James exhorts, Jude warns, and Jesus speaks of "this generation" and "the end of the age"—and in which Hebrews dares to say that in these last days, the God of Israel is still speaking, now in His Son, and inviting the whole world to become truly Hebrew in Him.

Appendix 2—How Covenant History Moves in Cycles

> *"Now these things happened to them as an example, but they were written down for our instruction, on whom the ends of the ages have come."*
>
> —1 CORINTHIANS 10:11

IN THIS BOOK, I insist that Jesus' words in Matthew 24 first addressed a real generation in real time—His own. "*This generation will not pass away*" is not a riddle; it is a warning fulfilled in the events of 66–70 CE when Jerusalem fell and the Temple burned. To ignore that is to sever Jesus from His own family and from the first hearers of His prophecy. But to say it happened then is not to say it is only about then.

The Bible rarely works in straight lines. It works in covenantal cycles. Deuteronomy, the Prophets, and even the Book of Revelation describe a recurring pattern:

- God forms a people and entrusts them with a vocation.
- That people drifts—into idolatry, compromise, or self-confidence in their own righteousness.
- Prophetic warning comes, often ignored or domesticated.
- A "day of the Lord" arrives—judgment, shaking, unveiling.
- And within the crisis, God preserves a remnant and opens a door of mercy.

The fall of Jerusalem in the first century is one such day. It is the climactic covenant crisis for the story Jesus' family was living in. Yet the pattern did not stop in 70 CE. The same covenant God, the same human heart, and the same spiritual forces mean that "last days" is not a calendar label so much as a recurring condition—those moments when God confronts a people who have forgotten why they were chosen in the first place.

This is why believers today can read Matthew 24 and honestly say, "*These are the last times; the Lord is coming soon.*" They are not entirely wrong. They are sensing that the church, like Israel before her, can drift into self-confidence, nationalism, and institutional religion while the poor weep and the nations rage. They feel the enemy not only in the streets but in the pulpits. What they often lack is the Jewish, covenantal story that shows how this fits the same pattern Scripture has traced for centuries. So, I will argue two things at once:

- Matthew 24 first spoke about Jesus' own generation and the destruction of Jerusalem.
- Yet its shape—its covenant logic, its birth pangs, its call to watchfulness—repeats in history wherever God's people forget whose story they are in.

We do not need a new prophecy chart. We need to recover the ancient pattern. Only then can we honor both the reality of what happened in the first century and the seriousness of the hour we are living in now.

Appendix 3—The Jews of Jesus' Day and Ours

A BASIC CATEGORY HELPS at the outset. "Hebrew" is the older covenant-line designation (Abram the Hebrew; the people who "crossed over"), while "Jew" is the later Judah-centered historical label—yet with deeper biblical resonance. In that sense, all Jews belong within the Hebrews of Scripture, though the biblical category "Hebrew" is broader than the later label "Jew." Keeping categories clean prevents covenant debates from collapsing into modern racial or political talk.

A second category matters just as much: "Jew/Judah" is praise-language before it is ideology. Judah's name is anchored in the verb *to praise/thank* (see Gen. 29:35). That means "Jewishness" is not first a racial slogan; it is a priestly vocation—a people called to praise the God of Israel and bear His name faithfully before the nations.

The New Testament reinforces this by describing Israel as the oracle-keepers. Paul can say that Israel's chief advantage is this: "they were entrusted with the oracles of God" (Rom. 3:2). Stephen speaks of Moses receiving "living oracles" to give to Israel (Acts 7:38). Hebrews assumes the same category when it rebukes sluggish disciples who still need "the basic principles of the oracles of God" (Heb. 5:12). Even Christian speech is to be patterned after this stewardship—"whoever speaks, as one who speaks oracles of God" (1 Pet. 4:11). Revelation, then, is not abstract information; it is entrusted speech, guarded and carried by a people. Mission must proceed with humility toward those to whom the oracles were first entrusted.

One further Pauline phrase must be handled with care, because it is often where modern "ethnic Israel" talk sneaks in. In Romans 9, Paul speaks of his "kinsmen according to the flesh" (*kata sarka*, Rom. 9:3–5). He is naming real genealogical and historical kinship—and he honors the covenant gifts bound up with Israel's story. But *kata sarka* is not a racial theory, and it is not an automatic eschatological mechanism. Paul's own guardrail is immediate: "not all who are descended from Israel belong to Israel" (Rom. 9:6). And in Romans 11, re-grafting is framed covenantally—"if they do not persist in unbelief" (Rom. 11:23)—while Gentiles are warned against boasting as though they had become the owners (Rom. 11:17–20). Paul affirms kinship without turning it into modern race-essence; he keeps mercy, faithfulness, and humility at the center.

It is also worth noting that Paul's *kata sarka* ("according to the flesh") sits close to the very place where covenant boundary markers were debated. "Flesh" is where circumcision is located, and circumcision was the flashpoint in first-century disputes about belonging. Still, Paul does not simply equate "according to the flesh" with "works of the law." The first names real kinship within Israel's historical people (Rom. 9:3–6); the second targets boundary practices when turned into badge-religion that fractures fellowship and treats Gentiles as second-class unless they adopt Jewish identity-markers (cf. Galatians; Rom. 3–4). Socially, the pressures overlap; theologically, the categories must be kept distinct.

The Jews in Jesus' Day: Judeans, Empire, and Contested Legitimacy

When the Gospels speak of "the Jews," especially in John, the phrase often functions less as a blanket ethnic term and more as a public-religious and political designation within a Roman imperial setting. In many scenes it points to the Judean establishment: those who speak with institutional authority, who represent the recognized religious order, and who have leverage under Roman oversight.

This is where modern readers easily misfire. "The Jews" in John does not mean "all Jewish people everywhere," and it certainly does not mean "Judaism as such." It often names the Judean leadership world in Jerusalem—frequently temple-adjacent, often boundary-policing, sometimes aligned with Sadducean interests, sometimes reflecting stricter halakhic instincts that later shorthand associates with Shammai. The conflicts are real, but they are intra-Jewish conflicts intensified by the pressures of empire.

Josephus helps us see how layered the word "Jew" could be in that period. In his descriptions of late Second Temple Judea, even Idumeans/

Edomites can be spoken of in Jewish terms because they are integrated into the Judean polity and its public religious identity. Whatever one concludes about the legitimacy of such integration, it warns the Christian reader not to treat "Jew" as a simple racial essence in the first century. In that world, the term is bound to Judea, polity, temple order, and contested communal boundaries—not to modern racial categories.

And the map matters. The New Testament assumes a world of distinctions: Judeans, Galileans, Samaritans, diaspora communities, and attached outsiders. Samaritans stand in a fraught kinship relation—close enough to share texts and claims, distant enough to preserve an alternative sacred geography and memory. Jesus' interactions across these boundaries expose the deeper issue: covenant fidelity and divine mercy are not reducible to badges of legitimacy.

Hebrews: Covenant Transition, Not People Replacement

Hebrews is often misread—not because its argument is unclear, but because inherited reflexes are strong. Many Christians have been trained to hear "new covenant" as "new people," and "obsolete" as "discarded." Hebrews never makes that leap.

Hebrews is emphatic that a covenant administration has reached its goal in Messiah. The Levitical priesthood, repeated sacrifices, and temple-centered mediation cannot remain the controlling framework for drawing near to God once Messiah has offered His once-for-all sacrifice (Heb. 7:23–28; 9:11–15, 24; 10:10–14, 18). Its pastoral spine is therefore simple and urgent: hold fast, draw near, and do not shrink back (Heb. 4:14–16; 10:22–25, 39; 12:1–3).

A single line prevents confusion: *Hebrews teaches covenant transition, not people replacement.*

The Lamb, Sacred Time, and the Shape of Fulfillment

Revelation speaks of "the Lamb slain from/before the foundation of the world" (Rev. 13:8). The theological force is clear: Messiah's sacrifice is not God's late adjustment after human failure, but the center of divine purpose from the beginning. Read that way, "new covenant" cannot mean a divine plan B in which God discards Israel and invents a different people. The "new" names fulfillment and access in Messiah, not a swap of identities.

This is also why Israel's covenant life is carried not only by texts but by time. The weekly Sabbath rhythm and the Hebrew calendar form a living pattern of remembrance and repentance. Passover and Yom Kippur stand across the year as covenant markers—deliverance and atonement—while Sabbath returns each week to rehearse holiness and hope. Read through that lived rhythm, Messiah's once-for-all sacrifice appears as fulfillment, not a late adjustment.

That is why Paul can say, "Messiah, our Passover, has been sacrificed" (1 Cor. 5:7). He is not creating a replacement story; he is locating Gentile believers inside Israel's redemption pattern—Passover, deliverance, covenant meal. The logic is grafting, not takeover (Rom. 11:17–20). Paul presses the same covenant logic into the Church's central act of worship: "This cup is the new covenant in my blood" (1 Cor. 11:25) is not "Israel canceled," but covenant access opened and sealed in Messiah, with Gentiles participating by grace in what God promised to Israel and Judah (Jer. 31:31; Heb. 8:8–12).

In synagogue-adjacent terms, it can be helpful to describe the Lord's Supper as Havdalah-shaped—not as if it is Havdalah, but as an analogy for what the meal does. Havdalah marks the transition from holy time to ordinary time; likewise, the Supper gathers the witnessing community, re-centers it on Messiah's once-for-all sacrifice, and sends it back into ordinary life with renewed identity and guarded holiness—without arrogance, because the pattern is Israel's and the mercy is shared by grafting (Rom. 11:17–20).

Jeremiah 31: Hebrews' Guardrail Against Replacement

Hebrews argues for the new covenant by quoting Jeremiah—and Jeremiah names the addressees without embarrassment: "the house of Israel and the house of Judah" (Jer. 31:31), cited directly in Hebrews (Heb. 8:8–12). Hebrews does not edit that line. That makes Jeremiah 31 a built-in guardrail: the new covenant is not God "moving on" after Israel or Judah failed, but Israel's promised renewal secured through Messiah's priesthood and sacrifice (Heb. 9:11–15; 10:15–18).

Ezrah and Ger: Covenant Membership and Covenant Fidelity

Here the Torah's own categories help Christian speech near the synagogue. In the Sinai vocabulary, Israel includes the *ezrah* (native-born) and the ger (sojourner/attached outsider). Torah repeatedly insists on a single covenant ethic of justice and holiness that embraces both—one worship of the God of Israel, one standard of righteousness.

Later Jewish practice adds further halakhic clarifications (including questions of lineage and conversion). But the covenant logic remains: status is never a substitute for faithfulness. Scripture warns against native-born presumption, and it honors the attached outsider who fears God. In that sense, it is better to be a faithful ger than an unfaithful *ezrah*—because the deepest issue is not badge or ancestry but walking in covenant truth.

This is precisely where Christian arrogance is exposed. If "Jew" is praise-language and priestly vocation, then any posture that treats Jews as disposable props—or treats Gentiles as the new owners—contradicts the very name. And if Sinai already makes room for ger and *ezrah* under one covenant God, then Gentile inclusion in Messiah must be framed as merciful attachment, not identity theft.

That is also why Acts and Galatians put such weight on table fellowship. Peter's struggle, Paul's confrontation, and Cornelius's inclusion are not marginal disputes about food; they reveal the covenant order of inclusion—Gentiles brought near without seizing Israel's name, received under Messiah's yoke, and taught a faithful way of life. Romans 11 manners belong at the table: humility, gratitude, and fear of arrogance (Rom. 11:17–20).

"Works of the Law," Pharisees, and Category Collapse

Pharisees emerge as a recognizable movement in the Second Temple struggle over covenant fidelity. In that context, Paul's phrase "works of the law" should not be flattened into "Torah is bad" or "Judaism is self-salvation." Often Paul is targeting boundary-marking, factional badge-wearing, or nominal religion that substitutes for the obedience of faith. None of that authorizes contempt for Torah—or contempt for Jews.

The Jews of Our Day: Modernity, Race-Talk, and Political Anachronism

A further distortion enters when Christians read modern categories back into the New Testament. In the modern West, especially in Europe, Jewish identity was increasingly spoken of in racial and nationalist terms as modernity reshaped how peoples imagined belonging. The language of "race," "blood," and "nation" became a dominant grammar for identity. Under those pressures—legal, social, cultural, and sometimes violent—Jewish communities faced a world that demanded new forms of political self-description.

This is where Christians must be careful. The "Jewish race" as a controlling explanatory category is a modern construct—a product of modern classification and nationalist imagination. It does not map cleanly onto biblical categories, and it does not map cleanly even onto European ethnic realities, where populations are visibly diverse within the same national name.

Within that modern climate, Zionism emerged as a nation-state project shaped by modern political instincts. Whatever one concludes about its arguments, its form belongs to the modern world: identity secured by statehood, vulnerability answered by borders, belonging stabilized through political sovereignty. That modern grammar should not be smuggled back into the New Testament as if it were the native covenant vocabulary of Scripture.

Christians therefore need a disciplined way to speak: not with denial of Jewish suffering, not with contempt for Jewish longing, and not with a naïve baptizing of modern political projects as if they were the kingdom of God.

Observant Jews Today: Speak with Accuracy and Honor

Many observant Jews know the New Covenant promise because it is not a Christian invention. It is Jeremiah's promise to Israel and Judah (Jer. 31:31–34). So, when Christians talk about Hebrews and "covenant transition," the pastoral application must not sound like: "Torah observance is obsolete." Hebrews targets temple-centered priestly mediation and repeated sacrifices as the basis of access to God—not Torah as covenant instruction, not Jewish identity, and not faithful practice as such (Heb. 7–10).

So:

- Don't treat Torah observance as "trying to earn salvation."
- Don't weaponize Hebrews against Jews.
- Name the shared anchor—Jeremiah 31—and speak with Romans 11 humility (Rom. 11:17–20).

If the gospel is entrusted speech, then Christian witness must sound like stewardship—not seizure. And if Jewishness is praise-language before it is ideology, then Christians should be the last people on earth to turn "the Jews" into a flattened label—whether for contempt, propaganda, or theological convenience.

Appendix 4—Beyond Full Preterism and Pure Futurism

In this book, I argue that Matthew 24 first speaks to a real generation in real time—Jesus' own. The fall of Jerusalem in 70 CE is a covenantal "day of the Lord," and we dishonor Jesus' words if we pretend His prophecy skipped over His first hearers and landed only on us.

But that is very different from saying that everything is finished and done.

Scripture does not end with 70 CE. Nor does Jewish hope. The biblical story, and the Jewish calendar that still shapes it, move toward what Israel calls *ha-ʿ olam ha-ba*—the world to come. However we line up our charts, the deep conviction is shared:

- History is going somewhere,
- judgment and mercy will be brought to light,
- and God's reign will be manifest in a renewed creation.

The New Testament speaks of this in its own language: the Great White Throne, the resurrection of the dead, the new heavens and new earth. However we frame the timing and the details, the core is clear:

- Jesus will come as the final Judge.
- There will be a public, universal judgment of the living and the dead.
- Death itself will be destroyed.
- Creation will be renewed, not discarded.

For that reason, I prefer not to speak only of a "first" and "second" coming as if Jesus were absent in the long stretch of history between them. He has come many times—even in the story of ancient Israel and before. He comes now. And He will come in a final way—a coming when every hidden thing is brought to light and God is "all in all."

When someone hears that Matthew 24 was fulfilled in the first century, the instinct is often to reach for a label: full preterist on one side, futurist on the other. Both can become flattening schemes. Full preterism tends to pull everything into the past: the coming of the Son of Man becomes only a metaphor for 70 CE; resurrection and judgment become purely symbolic; the world to come is reduced to inner experience or church history. Pure futurism, in reaction, pushes almost everything into the future: Matthew 24 becomes a codebook for our news cycle; the first-century audience becomes almost irrelevant; hope shrinks down to escaping the world rather than seeing it renewed. This book is trying to do something else:

- Honor the first-century fulfillment of Jesus' words in the life of His own family, His own people, and His own city.
- Recover the covenantal cycles Scripture describes—where judgment and mercy, shaking and renewal, recur whenever God calls His people to account.
- Keep alive the future hope that Israel has always carried: that God will judge in righteousness, raise the dead, and bring *olam ha-ba* in fullness.

I am not relocating the Kingdom into a closed past, nor postponing it into a distant future that excuses us from responsibility in the present. I am tracing how the Kingdom broke in then, confronts us now, and will be revealed in fullness at the final coming.

Olam Ha-Ba and Our Vocation as Living Temple

The Jewish language of *olam ha-zeh* (*this age*) and *olam ha-ba* (*the age to come*) reminds us that the transition is not passive. In God's mystery, the world to come is already breaking into this world as His people live out their vocation.

We are called to heal the world—to share in what later Jewish language calls tikkun—not as self-saviors, but as the living temple in whom His Spirit dwells. The same God who will one day renew all things has already taken up residence in His people, so that even now the life of the age to come leaks into the present age. So, to be plain:

- I affirm a real, future resurrection of the dead.
- I affirm a real, final judgment before God's throne.
- I affirm a real transition into a renewed creation, the *olam ha-ba* where righteousness dwells.

What I reject is not the final coming, but the prophecy industry and the flat schemes—whether full preterist or purely futurist—that turn every text into a code, or a living hope into nostalgia or terror, and forget the first-century family who first heard Jesus speak. Matthew 24 has a concrete fulfillment in that generation and a covenantal pattern that repeats—but the story does not end there. It bends toward the day when the One who judged Jerusalem will judge the nations, wipe away every tear, and bring the world to come in fullness through the very One who already dwells in us as His living temple. The Jesus His family knew will come again, and when He does, it will be the fulfillment of the mercy they sang, practiced, and defended—not the triumph of our charts.

Appendix 5—Relating to Muslims

Most Christians instinctively know there is a better way to speak with Muslims than either of the two defaults we keep falling into: combat or collapse. Combat treats the other as a threat to be defeated. Collapse treats the other as "basically the same," so that witness becomes embarrassment and conviction becomes impolite. Neither is faithful. The first hardens the heart; the second empties the Gospel of its substance.

There is a third way—older, quieter, and more demanding: confident witness without cultural war. Not pluralistic surrender, and not anxious posturing—rather, a life so anchored in Messiah the Restorer as they understand (see chapter 7) that it does not need to scapegoat, exaggerate, or perform. It can listen without flinching and speak without swagger. This posture does not panic when it meets real devotion outside the Church because it knows the difference between honoring a person and surrendering the claim of the Gospel. It is what a missionary tradition (Lesslie Newbigin above all) called a proper confidence: humility that can still make a claim, because the claim rests on God's faithfulness rather than our anxiety.

Holy Jealousy Is Covenant Language, Not Rivalry

This is where the biblical language of "jealousy" becomes unexpectedly helpful—provided we hear it the way Scripture means it. In the Song of Moses, God says: "*They have made me jealous with what is no god . . . so I will make them jealous with those who are not a people; I will provoke them to anger with a foolish nation*" (Deut. 32:21; echoed in Rom. 10:19 and developed in Rom. 11:11–14).

When Scripture speaks of jealousy, it is not petty insecurity. It is covenant language. The God of Israel is jealous the way a faithful spouse is jealous: not against the beloved, but for the beloved, when love and loyalty are being squandered.

But covenant jealousy must never be weaponized. It does not authorize contempt, scapegoating, or the old habit of treating other peoples as props in our fears. In Romans, the provocation of "jealousy" is not the humiliation of Israel; it is mercy moving outward to the nations in order to summon Israel inward again—grafting, not takeover (see Rom. 11:17–20).

And because Islam also claims Abraham, this theme should press Christians into deeper humility—not a surrender of conviction, but repentance. We do not "own" the God of Abraham. We bear witness to what we believe God has done in Jesus, while recognizing that many Muslims, in their own way, pursue reverence, prayer, fasting, and almsgiving—practices that can rebuke Christian hypocrisy without being the Gospel. So, we receive the rebuke as mercy, and we pray for the light of Messiah to open eyes—without resentment, and without retreat.

A Living Parable from Sweden

This is not theoretical for me. It has a date and a place: Living in Sweden. A moment from that season has stayed with me as a living parable of what "holy jealousy" is—and what it is not.

Our daughter fell off a horse, and for a terrifying stretch, she could not move her legs. She was taken to the hospital in Jönköping (the Swedes call it their "Jerusalem"), and we asked for prayer immediately—by telephone. We called a close friend (Latin American, married to a Swede), and she prayed with us right then, in the raw urgency of fear, asking the Lord for mercy.

At that same moment, our friend happened to be with a Muslim friend. And what unfolded there was quiet, unforced, and unforgettable. Our friend simply prayed—freely, naturally, without hesitation—thanking the Lord and interceding for our daughter. The Muslim woman was struck, not by rhetoric, not by argument, but by the ease of it: the plain confidence that God hears.

Our daughter recovered fully and had no lasting problems (though she never liked horses much after that). But what remained with me most was the shape of the moment: an unseen phone call, a prayer offered without performance, a Muslim friend watching a Christian speak to God as if God were near—and a family learning again that the center is not fear.

The center is Presence. And that is where covenant jealousy is meant to land—not in rivalry, suspicion, or hatred, but in reverent awakening: a life with God so real it becomes "provocation" in the best sense. It makes others wonder whether the living God is near, whether He listens, whether He might be faithful even now.

Acts 15, Amos 9, and the Horizon for Muslim Engagement

This comes to a head in James's speech at the Jerusalem Council (see Acts 15). Faced with the question of how Gentiles can enter the people of God without becoming Jews, James reaches back to Amos 9. The thrust is that when the fallen tent of David is raised, God's purpose is not small or tribal. It reaches outward—first to the estranged brother or the forgotten through Ishmael and then to the edges of humanity. However we map the textual details, the direction is clear: God is gathering "a people for His name" from among the nations in a way that does not erase Israel but fulfills the prophetic promise.

That is the horizon in which Muslims must be seen: heirs to a long, complicated conversation about Abraham, Ishmael, and the God who is One. If God's aim includes "the remnant of humanity" and "all the nations who are called by my name," then our stance toward Muslims cannot be one of cultural war, but of patient, hopeful witness.

Why Naming Debates Matter

Muslim memory and Muslim law also illustrate how names can solidify into "history." Labels that begin as descriptors can become protected categories—legal, communal, even sacred—and once that happens, polemics and survival pressures tend to harden identities over time. A name becomes a boundary marker; a boundary marker becomes a story; and eventually the story feels as immovable as the past itself.

The point is not to sneer at that reality, as if "they" are uniquely guilty of it. It is to learn humility. Christians should read naming disputes—ours and others'—with caution and restraint, especially when labels become weapons. Naming is never only about accuracy; it is also about power: who gets to define whom, who gets to belong, and whose memory is authorized.

Nowhere is this line-in-the-sand dynamic stronger, in modern Western Christianity, than in the way "the Muslim threat" has been narrated in all its dimensions—spiritual, cultural, political, and demographic. When fear becomes the lens, "Muslim" stops functioning as a complex human and religious descriptor and becomes a single charged symbol. At that point, language no longer helps us see; it helps us brace. It trains the soul to anticipate danger rather than to discern persons. And when that happens, Christians may think they are defending truth while they are actually being formed by anxiety—rehearsing old wounds and projecting them onto a whole people.

A more faithful posture begins by refusing to let labels do our moral thinking for us. It insists on precision, on patience, and on the discipline of distinguishing persons from polemics, neighbors from narratives, and actual doctrinal disagreements from the reflex to treat an entire community as a threat. That is not relativism. It is restraint. It is the refusal to let fear become our eschatology.

Living as a Witnessing Community Among Muslims

So how do we relate to Muslims considering all this?

- We do not come as conquerors. We come as a witnessing community—a people who live by mercy, not dominance.
- We let our life in Jesus be a jealousy-provoking sign in the best sense: communities where prayer is real, hospitality is practiced, truth is spoken without swagger, and compassion is not selective.

We remember that "jealousy" cuts toward our own house as well. Faithful Muslim devotion—reverence, fasting, prayer, and almsgiving—can expose Christian hypocrisy without being the Gospel. Many are sincerely seeking to honor God as they understand Him. A humble Christian response can receive the rebuke as mercy, pray for the light of Messiah to open eyes, and still bear witness to King Jesus without retreat or resentment.

In the end, this is not a technique for interfaith debate. It is a call to recover missionary realism: God has not given up on the nations. Our role is not to sit on top of the story, but to stand inside it—grateful, truthful, and steady—so that real conversation can begin where Scripture puts it: not in fear, but in the quiet provocation of a life lived before the living God.

Appendix 6—We Are All Prophets

"Your sons and your daughters shall prophesy"

—Joel 2:28

"The testimony of Jesus is the spirit of prophecy."

—Revelation 19:10

When Prophecy Became Fortune Telling

One of the most damaging reductions in modern Christianity is the idea that prophecy primarily means predicting the future. This assumption is so deeply embedded in evangelical culture that many believers cannot imagine prophecy functioning in any other way. As a result, prophecy has been handed over either to speculative chart-makers or to ministries obsessed with decoding headlines.

But this understanding would have been unintelligible to the biblical writers.

In Scripture, prophecy is not prediction first; it is confrontation. It is truth spoken into power. It is covenantal fidelity voiced in the presence of injustice. When future consequences are announced, they are not predictions for curiosity's sake, but warnings meant to provoke repentance. A prophet does not reveal secrets of the future. A prophet reveals reality as God sees it.

Elijah: The Prophet Who Refused Normalization

Elijah, the paradigmatic prophet, did not spend his ministry forecasting distant events. He confronted kings. He exposed false worship. He named injustice. He disrupted the illusion that Baal—and by extension, imperial power—was sustaining the world.

When Elijah declares drought, it is not a parlor trick or a magical act. It is covenantal judgment: a people who sever themselves from the Giver of rain cannot presume abundance. When he stands on Carmel, he does not predict the future; he forces a decision in the present. He tears away the veil. He makes the moment plain.

Elijah's prophetic power lies here: he refuses to allow injustice to normalize itself.

That is why Elijah becomes the template for later prophetic hope—not because he predicted well, but because he stood faithfully against a system that had baptized corruption as ordinary life.

"Are You Elijah?"—How a Vocation Becomes a People

When John the Baptist is asked whether he is Elijah, he says no.

When Jesus speaks of John, He says yes.

This is not contradiction; it is clarification.

John is not Elijah reincarnated. He does not carry Elijah's biography. But he stands in Elijah's vocation. He confronts Herod. He calls Israel back to covenant. He names corruption in religious and political leadership alike—and pays for it. With John, Elijah ceases to be a solitary figure and becomes a recognizable mode of faithfulness. With Jesus, that mode multiplies.

Pentecost and the End of Prophetic Elites

At Pentecost, Peter does not announce the arrival of new spiritual specialists. He announces the democratization of prophecy: "*Your sons and daughters shall prophesy . . . even on my servants, both men and women*" (Acts 2:17–18, NIV). This is not primarily about ecstatic speech. It is about a people trained to speak truth in a crooked world—people whose mouths are no longer owned by fear.

The New Testament does not imagine a church divided into prophets and non-prophets. It imagines a prophetic people, ordered by diverse gifts but united in testimony. Paul makes this explicit: "*You can all prophesy, one by one*" (1 Cor. 14:31).

Prophecy here is intelligible, accountable, and oriented toward the building up of the community. It is the speech of people who see clearly because they belong to the light.

Paul's Gifts: One Spirit, Many Forms, One Prophetic People

Here we must be careful—and Paul helps us be careful. Paul never creates a two-tier church: the "gifted" and the "ordinary." He creates something far more demanding: a body in which no one is unnecessary, no one is self-sufficient, and no one gets to confuse their function with their worth.

Across his letters, Paul gives multiple gift-lists (see Rom. 12; 1 Cor. 12–14; Eph. 4). They differ in wording because his point is not to hand us a closed inventory. His point is to show us what the Spirit does when Jesus forms a people:

- Romans 12 places gifts inside the logic of mercy and embodied service: prophecy, ministry, teaching, exhortation, giving, leading, mercy—gifts that look like a renewed mind and a living sacrifice.
- 1 Corinthians 12–14 places gifts inside the logic of love and ordered worship: wisdom, knowledge, faith, healings, miracles, prophecy, discernment, tongues, interpretation—gifts that must be practiced for edification, not status.
- Ephesians 4 places gifts inside the logic of maturity and unity: apostles, prophets, evangelists, shepherds, teachers—given so the saints are equipped, the Body is built up, and the Church grows into Christ.

What matters for our purpose is this: prophecy is one gift among many, but the prophetic vocation is shared by all. Not everyone has the same role. Not everyone carries the same assignment. Paul is explicit: "*Are all prophets?*"—meaning, are all appointed to the specific function of prophet in the body? No. Diversity is real; the body needs different organs.

And yet, Paul is also explicit that prophecy—understood as truth-bearing, Christ-witnessing speech for the sake of the community—must not be quarantined into a spiritual elite. He can say, without contradiction, both things at once:

- Not all are prophets in office or function.
- And yet the Church is to be a prophetic people—so that in the life of the Body, "*you can all prophesy . . . that all may learn and all be encouraged.*"

This is why Paul insists that prophecy be discerned ("weigh what is said"), that it be ordered ("one by one"), and that it be loving (without love, it becomes noise). Prophetic speech is not a license to perform intensity; it is a summons to costly clarity—truth that builds up, truth that exposes lies, truth that strengthens the weak, truth that refuses the intimidation of the age. In Paul, the gifts do not create spectators. They create participants—a whole community trained into faithful witness, with different graces, different emphases, different strengths, and one Lord.

Nebaioth: Prophecy Before the Prophets

Here the story reaches deeper still. Nebaioth—the firstborn of Ishmael—stands as a sign that blessing did not stop at Isaac's tent. God promised Ishmael fruitfulness and princes; Nebaioth is the first evidence of that promise taking historical shape (Gen. 17:20; 25:13). And his name—often associated with "utterances / speaking / prophetic voice," or with "heights / prominence"—places *speech before God* inside Abraham's wider family line, long before Israel develops a public prophetic class.

But Nebaioth matters for another reason—one that reads like a midrash of hope. Esau's "outside marriage" was never simply an ethnic detail; it is a *family-theology signal.* When Esau takes Mahalath, daughter of Ishmael (and thus a kin-daughter of Abraham's household), Genesis quietly shows a door reopening: Esau is pulled back toward Abraham's family orbit through Ishmael's line (Gen. 28:9; cf. 36:3). In that light, Nebaioth is not only Ishmael's firstborn; he becomes a hinge-point in the story of fraternal repair—*a firstborn who helps a firstborn come home.*

And then the name keeps traveling. Second Temple-era writers already associated Nebaioth with the Nabataeans—the desert trading peoples whose world stretched through Arabia Petraea and whose famous center was Petra. Josephus (and later Jerome) explicitly make that identification, and modern reference works still register it—while also admitting the linguistic/philological questions that make the equation debated.

This is where the grafting-in theme lands with weight: in the Second Temple period, "Edom" did not remain a sealed-off other. Idumeans/Edomites were incorporated into Judean life under the Hasmoneans (however one judges the means and the morality of that incorporation), and the region's "Abrahamic border peoples" increasingly lived in and around Israel's covenant-world.

So Nebaioth reminds us that prophecy is not a late religious specialization. It is an ancient human vocation—bearing witness before heaven and earth—present already in Abraham's extended household. Israel does not invent prophecy; Israel guards and disciplines it within covenant, so that the fire is not turned into pagan frenzy or imperial speechcraft. In the New Testament, that guarded fire is released again—not to replace Israel, but to extend Israel's light outward, gathering the families of the earth the way Genesis always promised.

The Testimony of Jesus

Revelation offers the simplest and most unsettling definition of prophecy: "*The testimony of Jesus is the spirit of prophecy*" (Rev. 19:10). That line strips prophecy down to the bone. Prophecy isn't a codebook. It isn't insider information. It isn't religious performance dressed up as certainty. Prophecy is witness.

To testify to Jesus—to the way He lives, the Kingdom He announces, the way He exposes false power, the way He judges injustice without becoming unjust Himself, the way He refuses violence even when violence closes in—that is prophecy. And that is why the Early Church collides with empire almost immediately. Not because Christians were looking for a fight, but because faithful witness always threatens systems built on fear, coercion, and managed truth.

That's also why martyrdom and prophecy keep showing up together. When the world demands your silence, and you keep speaking—quietly, steadily, truthfully—that costs something. And the cost is the point. Prophecy is not always loud. Prophecy is not primarily predictive. Prophecy is costly clarity.

We Are All Prophets, Elijah

Here's the claim that unsettles modern Christianity the most: Not that everyone can "foretell." Not that everyone is a pulpit preacher. But that every baptized believer is pulled into Elijah's kind of vocation—a life that refuses to bend the knee to lies. To be an Elijah-person is:

- to refuse convenient falsehoods,
- to name injustice without needing permission,
- to bear witness in a world that rewards silence,
- to speak the truth without trying to control the outcome.

Some do that through teaching, serving, hospitality and endurance—through suffering that refuses to become bitter or cruel. But all do it the same way: by belonging to the One Revelation calls the Faithful Witness. The Church doesn't need more prophecy charts. It needs more people who realize they are already standing in a prophetic calling because they are already bound to Jesus. And it starts here: Prophecy isn't about seeing the future. It's about telling the truth—now.

Closing Thought—The Celestial City and the Healed Temple

This book has argued that the last days are not an escape plan but a covenantal summons: to walk in the Name, to refuse counterfeit kingdoms, and to live now as citizens of the city that is coming. But that summons always meets resistance—not only from overt falsehood, but from the subtler counterfeit that feels holy because it sounds like longing.

Every generation gets its eschatology from somewhere. Some of it comes from pulp prophecy, some from politics, and some—more than we like to admit—comes from the songs and images that discipled our imaginations before we had words for what we were feeling. If the last days are a vocation rather than a riddle, then we must tell the truth about the rival liturgies that trained our hopes and fears.

That is why counterfeits matter. They do not merely misinform; they form. They train the heart to discern for a Kingdom. And in my generation, one of the most vivid parables of a manufactured "messiah"—beautiful, magnetic, finally devouring—came to us in the strange liturgy of David Bowie's Ziggy Stardust—that apocalyptic glam mythology of a "messiah" manufactured by spectacle: dazzling, androgynous, and finally cut off from his Creator by his own devices.

Ziggy isn't simply rebellious; he's liturgical in his own way—an altar built to the self. He doesn't merely perform; he invites devotion. The crowd's hunger for transcendence is answered, not by repentance or covenantal fidelity, but by a new kind of worship: self as savior, image as glory, charisma as authority. A creature takes the stage and—without ever saying the words—claims the place of the One who made him.

But for Cleveland, Bowie wasn't just an odd British import. Cleveland mattered in the Ziggy story. The first U.S. Ziggy show opened at Cleveland Music Hall on September 22, 1972, and it sold out quickly helped along by the way our iconic radio station WMMS played Bowie's music, creating a fan base before the rest of America caught up. In that sense, Bowie wasn't simply on Cleveland radio; for many of us, he felt like a kind of local "rock god"—the soundtrack of a city that knew it was hearing something new in Rock music and where the label was coined.

Beside Mick Ronson's guitar—which captivated me more than Bowie's persona—there was "Five Years": that opening alarm bell, the whole record set to a countdown, apocalypse translated into pop drama. Time is running out, and the world feels suddenly thin.

But after that comes "Starman." Only years later did I realize how deeply it echoes the Christian imagination—the ache for a world made whole, the longing for the One whose appearing will set all things right. The line held a truth I didn't yet know how to name: the world is wounded, but Someone is coming. Our work of repair—what Jewish tradition calls *tikkun olam*—matters, not as the trigger for His appearing, but as the practiced loyalty of a people learning to live toward the world, He will finish healing yet also much through our collective cooperation.

And Bowie's reach didn't stop with my generation. U2 have repeatedly nodded toward him, even dedicating *Songs of Experience* in part to the "teenage dreams of David Bowie." That's the strange thing about cultural artifacts: even when the theology is confused, the human ache can still be real. A false "star" can still accidentally point toward the true light.

That's what the Gospel refuses: spectacle as salvation. And that's why A. B. Simpson's "bring back the King" is the opposite of escapism—it's apprenticeship in the true Kingdom. A century ago, Simpson grasped that truth, not as an escape fantasy but a summons to mission and mercy. He believed that to long for Christ's appearing was to live now in the power of the age to come, to carry His compassion into the nations.

The Student Volunteer Movement heard the same call. Their eschatology was not fear-driven or speculative; it was participatory, not simply the Gospel in word but in deed. They believed that God had entrusted His people with a role in the healing of the world—an eschatology of responsibility, not resignation. They knew what the prophets knew: that history is full of competing gods. As Micah 4:5 says: "*For all the peoples walk, each in the name of its god; but we will walk in the name of the LORD our God forever and ever.*" People will walk after many gods—national, political, ideological, technological.

- The future will never lack idols.
- But the remnant walks differently.
- The remnant walks in the Name.

And the only ones who can walk that way are those who have learned humility. This is why counterfeit "stars" matter: they train the heart for a kingdom. The only question is which kingdom.

And that question is not left vague in the teaching of Jesus. In Matthew 25, when the Son of Man comes in glory and separates the sheep from the goats, He does not interrogate the nations about their prophetic timelines. He asks about their faithfulness to His hidden presence—the way their hope took on flesh in the ordinary places where the Kingdom is either received or refused. "*I was hungry . . . I was thirsty . . . I was a stranger . . . naked . . . sick . . . in prison . . .* " *and then the unsettling refrain: "as you did it to one of the least of these . . . you did it to me*" (Matt. 25:35–40).

The shock of the scene is that both groups are surprised. The sheep did not know they were serving Him. The goats did not know they were neglecting Him. That is the point: the last days are not primarily a riddle to solve but a vocation to inhabit. The King judges history by whether we learned to recognize His face when it came without spectacle, without leverage, without the aura of importance—whether we were trained by rival liturgies to chase shining counterfeits, or trained by covenant humility to move toward the wounded.

Matthew 25, then, is not a distraction from eschatology; it is eschatology's moral and covenantal core. It reveals what it means to "walk in the Name" when the future is crowded with idols. The remnant walks differently not because it has superior information, but because it has been apprenticed into the manners of the coming Kingdom. Their longing is not merely verbal; it becomes a modus operandi: mercy toward the least, faithfulness under pressure, courage without conquest. Not as the trigger for His appearing, but as the practiced loyalty of a people learning to live now toward the world He will finish healing—yet also much through our collective cooperation.

In this light, the Sheep and the Goats is a bridge into Revelation's descending city. The New Jerusalem is not a reward for those who guessed correctly, but the healed Temple-world prepared for those who learned, by the

Spirit, how to live toward the King's hidden presence. The city that comes down is previewed in lives that "live downward" now—toward strangers, prisoners, the sick, the overlooked, the inconvenient. The Gospel refuses spectacle as salvation, and it also refuses the lie that we can love the coming King while ignoring the places where He has chosen to be encountered.

The City That Descends

Revelation's celestial city isn't a Christian escape hatch; it's the Temple story brought to its final healed form. When John sees the New Jerusalem, he does not watch the Church "go up" into heaven. He sees the holy city coming down out of heaven from God (see Rev. 21:2). Heaven and Earth are not torn apart forever; they are finally married. The city is a bride, not a fortress: relational, covenantal, radiant with a beauty that comes from being loved and healed.

Its shape is not random. The city is a perfect cube—twelve thousand stadia in length, width, and height (see Rev. 21:16)—an echo of the Holy of Holies, the innermost room of the tabernacle and Temple where heaven and Earth already met in a concentrated way. Scaled out, John's vision describes something enormous, almost the size of a small moon. But he is not giving us an orbital diagram so that we can look for a glowing cube in deep space. He is showing us, in Temple geometry, what it means for God's presence to fill all creation: the holiness that once rested in a hidden inner room will one day encompass the whole cosmos. Revelation's cube-city is not an escape pod for a few, but the final, healed dwelling of God with humanity—a physical reality transfigured by glory.

There is "no temple" in the city, not because worship is abolished, but because "*its temple is the Lord God the Almighty and the Lamb*" (Rev. 21:22). What was once localized in Zion's inner room now fills the cosmos. The city is profoundly Jewish and irreducibly familial. Its gates carry the names of the twelve tribes of Israel; its foundations bear the names of the twelve apostles of the Lamb (see Rev. 21:12–14). The whole redeemed people of God is inscribed into its architecture: Israel and the ekklesia, root and branches, reunited in stone and light. The river of life flows from the throne, the tree of life straddles it, and the leaves are "*for the healing of the nations*" (see Rev. 22:1–2). The nations do not disappear. They walk in the Lamb's light. They bring their glory into the city. What began at Jacob's well with a Samaritan woman reaches its final horizon: estranged families healed, rival stories finally reconciled.

Read in this light, Revelation's celestial city is the same "Jerusalem above" Paul glimpses and the same motherly reality Mary prefigures. Mary carries the Messiah in her body for a time; the New Jerusalem carries the whole reconciled family of Abraham forever. Mary stands beneath the cross as "woman"; the city descends as the completed Bride. Both are images of a single mercy: God refusing to abandon His creation, His covenants, or His wounded children.

For eschatology, this changes everything. The goal is not evacuation to a distant realm but the descent of God's own life into a renewed world. The celestial city is not a gated community for the few; it is the consummation of every promise sung in the Magnificat, preached by James, guarded by Jude, and embodied by Jesus—the Father's face shining openly, the nations healed, Israel honored, and the family finally gathered home.

Whether we picture the New Jerusalem as a moon-sized city in orbit, a descending temple-mountain, or a reality that folds dimensions we barely have words for, Scripture's claim is stubbornly concrete: a city comes down. Zion is not an escape hatch from creation but God's way of bringing creation to its goal. The "Jerusalem above" is not a private devotion or a metaphor for inward spirituality; it is the promised dwelling of God with humanity, measured in real space, rooted in real covenant, arriving in real history. If its dimensions stretch our imagination to the scale of a small moon, perhaps that is the point: to break our addiction to tiny gospels and thin hopes. The story does not end with us going up to a disembodied heaven, but with a city coming down—a celestial Zion joining heaven and Earth—summoning Jews and nations alike to live now as citizens of a Kingdom whose capital already exists and is on its way.

In the end, that is what this whole book has been about. Not a past we can fully chart or a future we can fully map, but a living Messiah who has come since His Spirit hovered over the deep; who touched the Second Adam; who sat with Abraham as Three and saw the plight of Hagar, the mother of the patriarch's firstborn, Ishmael; who appeared again and again as the Angel of the Lord and the Word; who spoke from the bush that burned and was not consumed; who went before Israel in the cloud by day and the pillar of fire by night; who has met saints in visions and even Muslims, startled by the quiet mercy of a dream; who has appeared in many other theophanies—and who keeps coming, and who will come in fullness to make His Father's house—Abba's city—the home of all who love Him.

Full preterism flattens that hope into a closed past; pure futurism postpones it into a distant someday. The New Testament, read with Jesus' family, does something different. It teaches us to live now as citizens of the city that is coming—to let the life of the age to come leak into this age through mercy, fidelity, and courage.

The Last Days, in that light, are not a riddle to solve but a vocation to inhabit: to bear witness, as Mary, James, and Jude did, until the day when the Starman who once walked the roads of Galilee is revealed as the King whose face lights the streets of the New Jerusalem—and the earth is finally filled with the knowledge of the glory of the LORD as the waters cover the sea.

The Regions Beyond

Albert B. Simpson (1904)—Public Domain

1. To the regions beyond I must go, I must go,
Where the story has never been told;
To the millions that never have heard of His love,
I must tell the sweet story of old.

Refrain:

To the regions beyond I must go, I must go,
Till the world, all the world,
His salvation shall know.

2. To the hardest of places He calls me to go,
Never thinking of comfort or ease;
The world may pronounce me a dreamer, a fool,
Enough if the Master I please.

(Refrain)

3. Oh, you that are spending your leisure and pow'rs
In those pleasures so foolish and fond;
Awake from your selfishness, folly and sin,
And go to the regions beyond.

(Refrain)

4. There are other "lost sheep" that the Master must bring,
And to them must the message be told;
He sends me to gather them out of all lands,
And welcome them back to His fold.

(Refrain)

Recommended Reading

Jewish Voices Who Stretch Us and Clarify

Abrahamson, Ben (https://www.alsadiqin.org/en/index.php). Essays and research on Judaism, Islam, and shared covenantal history; online publications and reprints of Elijah Benamozegh.

Abrahamson, Ben. *People of the Table: Original Christianity*. AlSadiqin Institute, 2025.

Benamozegh, Elijah. *Israel and Humanity*. Translated by Maxwell Luria. Mahwah, NJ: Paulist Press, 1995.

Falk, Harvey. *Jesus the Pharisee: A New Look at the Jewishness of Jesus*. Eugene, OR: Wipf & Stock, 2005 (reprint of 1985 edition).

Kinzer, Mark S. *Postmissionary Messianic Judaism: Redefining Christian Engagement with the Jewish People*. Grand Rapids: Brazos Press, 2005.

Kinzer, Mark S. *Jerusalem Crucified, Jerusalem Risen: The Resurrected Messiah, the Jewish People, and the Land of Promise*. Grand Rapids, MI: Eerdmans, 2018.

Levenson, Jon D. *Sinai and Zion: An Entry into the Jewish Bible*. Minneapolis: Winston, 1985.

Levine, Amy-Jill. *The Misunderstood Jew: The Church and the Scandal of the Jewish Jesus*. New York: HarperOne, 2006.

Wyschogrod, Michael. *The Body of Faith: God in the People Israel*. New York: Seabury, 1983; new edition Lanham, MD: Rowman & Littlefield, 1996.

Yossi (Jo) "Pettur Chamor" WikiNoah.org
Online repository preserving early Jewish frameworks regarding Jesus,
the Desposyni, the Teliya tradition, and ancient Noachide teachings.
https://www.wikinoah.org/en/index.php/Category:Petter_Chamor_Approach
https://www.noahidejudaism.schule/
https://www.messianiclambradio.com/shows/petterchamor

What is the Gospel Evangelion https://www.wikinoah.org/en/index.php/Evangelion

Jewish Dialog with the Nations https://www.wikinoah.org/en/index.php/Bei_Abedan

Yeshua Sar Haphanim https://www.wikinoah.org/en/index.php/Yeshua

The Teliya https://www.wikinoah.org/en/index.php?title=Teliya_Ye.Sh.U.&redirect=no

Notzrim https://www.wikinoah.org/en/index.php/Notzrim

Saint Murad's Quran Translation

https://www.patreon.com/SaintMurad/shop/complete-package-quran-saint-murad-315350

https://buymeacoffee.com/saintmurad/official-quran-saint-murad-translation?utm_source=chatgpt.com

For the Wounded, Deconstructing, and Weary

Swoboda, A. J. *After Doubt: How to Question Your Faith Without Losing It.* Grand Rapids: Brazos, 2021.

Langberg, Diane. *Redeeming Power: Understanding Authority and Abuse in the Church.* Grand Rapids: Brazos, 2020.

Fitch, David E. *The Church of Us vs. Them: Freedom from a Faith That Feeds on Making Enemies.* Grand Rapids: Brazos, 2019.

Alliance Story, Mission, and the Kingdom

Simpson, A. B. *The Fourfold Gospel.* Camp Hill, PA: Christian Publications, various reprints.

Pyles, Franklin, and Lee Beach. *The Whole Gospel for the Whole World: Experiencing the Fourfold Gospel Today.* Eugene, OR: Pickwick, 2016.

Henry, Daryn R. *A. B. Simpson and the Making of Modern Evangelicalism.* Montreal/Kingston: McGill–Queen's University Press, 2019.

Jones, David P. *A. B.: The Unlikely Founder of a Global Movement.* Colorado Springs: The Christian and Missionary Alliance, 2022.

King, Paul L. *Anointed Women: The Rich Heritage of Women in Ministry in The Christian and Missionary Alliance.* Tulsa: Word & Spirit Press, 2009.

Fitch, David E. *Faithful Presence: Seven Disciplines That Shape the Church for Mission.* Downers Grove, IL: IVP Academic, 2016.

Continuing the Conversation

My Blog—"Gimme That Old Time Relationship"
https://globalsouthadvance.blogspot.com

Conversations with Yossi (Jo)
https://www.youtube.com/@fahznab

Bibliography

Abrahamson, Ben. *Confrontation and Engagement: Multi-Covenantalism in Orthodox Judaism—Meta-Halakhah, Rationalism, and Mysticism*. Jerusalem: Al-Sadiqin, 2024.

———. *People of the Table: Original Christianity*. Jerusalem: Al-Sadiqin, 2025.

Abulafia, Abraham. *Sefer Ha-Ot: The Book of the Sign*. PDF. Bet Emunah website. Accessed January 2026.

Arie, Eran, Baruch Rosen, and Dvory Namdar. "Cannabis and Frankincense at the Judahite Shrine of Arad." *Tel Aviv* 47, no. 1 (2020): 5–28.

Augustine. *The City of God*. Translated by Marcus Dods. In *Nicene and Post-Nicene Fathers*, First Series, vol. 2, edited by Philip Schaff. Buffalo, NY: Christian Literature, 1887.

———. *Contra Faustum Manichaeum*. In *Nicene and Post-Nicene Fathers*, First Series, vol. 4, edited by Philip Schaff. Peabody, MA: Hendrickson, 1994.

Banzhaf, Martin L. "Diaspora Movement through A. B. Simpson and His Beloved Disciple Michele Nardi (1850–1914): The Italian Evangelist." In *History, Theology and Mission of the C&MA (Proceedings of the Alliance Theological Symposium, Toulouse, June 2023)*, 39–47.

Barnes, Marc, and Robert A. Keefe. "A Tale of Two Jacks: C. S. Lewis and the Jews." *Public Discourse*, September 16, 2025.

Barth, Karl. *Church Dogmatics*. Vol. II/2. Edited by G. W. Bromiley and T. F. Torrance. Edinburgh: T&T Clark, 1957.

Bates, Matthew W. *Beyond the Salvation Wars: Why Both Protestants and Catholics Must Reimagine How We Are Saved*. Grand Rapids, MI: Brazos, 2025.

Bauckham, Richard. *Jude and the Relatives of Jesus in the Early Church*. Edinburgh: T&T Clark, 1990.

———. *Jude, 2 Peter*. Word Biblical Commentary 50. Waco, TX: Word Books, 1983.

Benamozegh, Elijah. *Israel and Humanity*. Translated by Maxwell Luria. New York: Paulist, 1995.

Boyer, Paul. *When Time Shall Be No More: Prophecy Belief in Modern American Culture*. Cambridge, MA: Harvard University Press, 1992.

Boyarin, Daniel. *The Jewish Gospels: The Story of the Jewish Christ*. New York: New Press, 2012.

Brown, Raymond E. *The Birth of the Messiah: A Commentary on the Infancy Narratives in the Gospels of Matthew and Luke*. Updated ed. New York: Doubleday, 1993.

Bunyan, John. *The Pilgrim's Progress*. London: Nathaniel Ponder, 1678.

Busch, Wilhelm. *Sämtliche Werke*. Edited by Otto Nöldeke. 8 vols. Munich: Braun & Schneider, 1943.

Casal, Xus. "Yeshua Sar haPanim in the Machzor for Yom Kippur." 13 Petals, 2015. https://www.13petals.org/topical-studies/shar-hapanim-in-the-machzor-for-yom-kippur/

Charlesworth, James H., ed. *The Old Testament Pseudepigrapha*. Vol. 1. Garden City, NY: Doubleday, 1983.

Chaucer, Geoffrey. *The Canterbury Tales*. Harvard's Geoffrey Chaucer Website. https://chaucer.fas.harvard.edu.

Davidson, Herbert A. *Moses Maimonides: The Man and His Works*. New York: Oxford University Press, 2005.

De Chirico, Leonardo. *Evangelical Theological Perspectives on Post–Vatican II Roman Catholicism*. Religions and Discourse 19. Oxford: Peter Lang, 2003.

De Chirico, Leonardo, Skyler S. Hamilton, and Joshua D. Cheney, eds. *Fully Roman Catholic: Pope Francis in Protestant Perspective: A Selection of Articles*. Eugene, OR: Wipf & Stock, 2025.

Deutsch, M. "The Strasbourg Manuscript of *Ma'aseh Talui*." *Proceedings of the American Academy for Jewish Research* (1966). https://www.wikinoah.org/en/index.php/%D7%AA%D7%9C%D7%99%D7%99%D7%AA_%D7%99%D7%A9%D7%95

Eckhart, Meister. *The Complete Mystical Works of Meister Eckhart*. Translated and edited by Maurice O'C. Walshe. Revised with a foreword by Bernard McGinn. New York: Crossroad, 2009.

Eusebius of Caesarea. *Ecclesiastical History*. Translated by Arthur Cushman McGiffert. In *Nicene and Post-Nicene Fathers*, Second Series, vol. 1, edited by Philip Schaff and Henry Wace. Buffalo, NY: Christian Literature, 1890.

Evangelische Kirche in Deutschland. "Theological Declaration of Barmen." https://www.ekd.de/en/the-barmen-declaration-303.htm

Falk, Harvey. *Jesus the Pharisee: A New Look at the Jewishness of Jesus*. Mahwah, NJ: Paulist, 1985.

———. "Rabbi Jacob Emden's Views on Christianity and the Noachide Commandments." *Journal of Ecumenical Studies* 19, no. 1 (Winter 1982): 105–111.

———. *Jesus the Pharisee: A New Look at the Jewishness of Jesus*. Eugene, OR: Wipf & Stock, 2003.

Firestone, Reuven. *Journeys in Holy Lands: The Evolution of the Abraham–Ishmael Legends in Islamic Exegesis*. Albany, NY: State University of New York Press, 1990.

Fisch, Yael. *Written in the Book of the Living: Understanding the Qur'an through Biblical Resonances*. Boston: Academic Studies, 2024.

Flusser, David. *Jewish Sources in Early Christianity*. New York: Adama, 1987.

Fredriksen, Paula. *Augustine and the Jews: A Christian Defense of Jews and Judaism*. New Haven: Yale University Press, 2010.

———. *When Christians Were Jews: The First Generation*. New Haven: Yale University Press, 2018.

Frykholm, Amy Johnson. *Rapture Culture: Left Behind in Evangelical America*. Oxford: Oxford University Press, 2004.

Garrett, Susan R. *No Ordinary Angel: Celestial Spirits and Christian Claims about Jesus*. Minneapolis: Fortress, 2008.

Green, Joel B. *The Gospel of Luke*. New International Commentary on the New Testament. Grand Rapids, MI: Eerdmans, 1997.

Griffith, Sidney H. *The Bible in Arabic: The Scriptures of the "People of the Book" in the Language of Islam*. Princeton, NJ: Princeton University Press, 2013.

Hays, Richard B. *Echoes of Scripture in the Letters of Paul*. New Haven, CT: Yale University Press, 1989.

Heiser, Michael S. *Reversing Hermon: Enoch, the Watchers, and the Forgotten Mission of Jesus Christ*. Bellingham, WA: Lexham, 2017.

———. *The Unseen Realm: Recovering the Supernatural Worldview of the Bible*. Bellingham, WA: Lexham, 2015.

Howe, Julia Ward. "The Battle Hymn of the Republic" ("Mine Eyes Have Seen the Glory"). *The Atlantic Monthly* 9, no. 52 (February 1862): 10.

Inbari, Motti, and Kirill Bumin. *Christian Zionism in the Twenty-First Century: American Evangelical Opinion on Israel*. Oxford: Oxford University Press, 2023.

Johnson, Luke Timothy. *The Letter of James*. Anchor Yale Bible 37A. New Haven, CT: Yale University Press, 1995.

Josephus. *Jewish Antiquities*. Translated by H. St. J. Thackeray, Ralph Marcus, Allen Wikgren, and Louis H. Feldman. Loeb Classical Library. Cambridge, MA: Harvard University Press, 1926–1965.

———. *The Jewish War*. Translated by H. St. J. Thackeray. Loeb Classical Library. Cambridge, MA: Harvard University Press, 1927–1928.

Kaiser, Walter C., Jr. "Israel's Missionary Call." In *Perspectives on the World Christian Movement: A Reader*, edited by Ralph D. Winter and Steven C. Hawthorne, 10–16. Pasadena, CA: William Carey Library, 2003.

Kelly, J. N. D. *Early Christian Doctrines*. Rev. ed. San Francisco: HarperOne, 1978.

Kimelman, Reuven. "Birkat Ha-Minim and the Lack of Evidence for an Anti-Christian Jewish Prayer in Late Antiquity." In *Jewish and Christian Self-Definition*, vol. 2, edited by E. P. Sanders et al. Philadelphia: Fortress, 1981.

King, Paul L. *Living in the Border Zone: The Collected Writings of A. B. Simpson on Kingdom and Not Fully Yet*. Kindle. Self-published, 2025.

Kistemaker, Simon J. *Revelation*. New Testament Commentary. Grand Rapids, MI: Baker Academic, 2001.

Knust, Jennifer Wright, and Tommy Wasserman. *To Cast the First Stone: The Transmission of a Gospel Story*. Princeton, NJ: Princeton University Press, 2019.

———. "The Pericope of the Adulteress (John 7:53–8:11): A Theory of Its Textual Transmission." *Svensk Exegetisk Årsbok* 85 (2020): 22–55.

Koester, Craig R. *Revelation: A New Translation with Introduction and Commentary*. Anchor Yale Bible 38A. New Haven, CT: Yale University Press, 2014.

———. "Revelation Numbers: Decoding 666, Seven Churches, and Biblical Symbols." *Enter the Bible*. https://enterthebible.org/audio/8-156-revelation-numbers-decoding-666-seven-churches-and-biblical-symbols-with-biblical-scholar-craig-koester.

Langer, Ruth. *Cursing the Christians? A History of the Birkat HaMinim*. New York: Oxford University Press, 2012.

Laughlin, Peter R. "Reframing Missionary Eschatology for the Global Alliance." In *Advancing the Vision: The Fourfold Gospel in Contemporary and Global Contexts*, edited by Bernie A. Van De Walle, Benjamin Elliott, Jenny-Lyn de Klerk, and Jura Yanagihara, 249–275. Eugene, OR: Pickwick, 2023.

Lewis, C. S. *Mere Christianity*. New York: Macmillan, 1952.

Longenecker, Richard N. *Biblical Exegesis in the Apostolic Period*. 2nd ed. Grand Rapids, MI: Eerdmans, 1999.

Luomanen, Petri. *Recovering Jewish Christian Sects and Gospels*. Leiden: Brill, 2012.

Luther, Martin. "Preface to the Epistles of St. James and St. Jude." In *Luther's Works*, vol. 35, *Word and Sacrament I*, edited by E. Theodore Bachmann. Philadelphia: Fortress, 1960.

Martyn, Sam. "The Role of Pre-Conversion Dreams and Visions in Islam: Evidence . . . " *Southeastern Theological Review* 9, no. 2 (Fall 2018): 57–66.

Mathison, Keith A. *Dispensationalism: Rightly Dividing the People of God?* Phillipsburg, NJ: P&R, 1995.

Meerson, Michael, and Peter Schäfer, eds. and trans. *Toledot Yeshu: The Life Story of Jesus: Two Volumes and Database. Vol. 1, Introduction and Translation; Vol. 2, Critical Edition*. Texts and Studies in Ancient Judaism 159. Tübingen: Mohr Siebeck, 2014.

Mohler, Al, Jr. "Have We Really Misunderstood the Gospel for 2,000 Years?" May 6, 2025. https://albertmohler.com/2025/05/06/have-we-really-misunderstood-the-gospel-for-2000-years/.

Moo, Douglas J. *The Letter of James*. Pillar New Testament Commentary. Grand Rapids: Eerdmans, 2021.

Mouriquand, David. "'Depravity and Lawlessness': U2 Speak Out on Israel's Actions in Gaza." *Euronews*, August 11, 2025. https://www.euronews.com/culture/2025/08/11/depravity-and-lawlessness-u2-speak-out-on-israels-actions-in-gaza.

Nanos, Mark D. *The Mystery of Romans: The Jewish Context of Paul's Letter*. Minneapolis: Fortress, 1996.

Neusner, Jacob. *The Documentary Foundation of Rabbinic Culture: Mopping Up After Debates with Gerald L. Bruns, S. J. D. Cohen, Arnold Maria Goldberg, Susan Handelman, Christine Hayes, James Kugel, Peter Schäfer, Eliezer Segal, E. P. Sanders, and Lawrence H. Schiffman*. South Florida Studies in the History of Judaism 113. Atlanta, GA: Scholars, 1995.

Nickelsburg, George W. E. *1 Enoch 1: A Commentary on the Book of 1 Enoch, Chapters 1–36; 81–108*. Hermeneia. Minneapolis: Fortress, 2001.

Nirenberg, David. *Anti-Judaism: The Western Tradition*. New York: Norton, 2013.

Paddison, Angus. "Karl Barth's Theological Exegesis of Romans 9–11 in the Light of Jewish–Christian Understanding." *Journal for the Study of the New Testament* 28, no. 4 (June 2006): 469–488. https://doi.org/10.1177/0142064X06065695.

Padilla DeBorst, Ruth. "Walking Humbly with God." Plenary address, Fourth Lausanne Congress, Incheon/Seoul, September 23, 2024. Lausanne Movement video archive.

Pelikan, Jaroslav. *Mary Through the Centuries: Her Place in the History of Culture*. New Haven: Yale University Press, 1996.

Pitre, Brant J. *Jesus and the Jewish Roots of Mary: Unveiling the Mother of the Messiah*. New York: Image, 2018.

Pritz, Ray A. *Nazarene Jewish Christianity: From the End of the New Testament Period Until Its Disappearance in the Fourth Century*. Studia Post-Biblica 37. Jerusalem: Magnes Press, Hebrew University; Leiden: Brill, 1988.

Pummer, Reinhard. *The Samaritans: A Profile*. Grand Rapids, MI: Eerdmans, 2016.

Purvis, James D. *The Samaritan Pentateuch and the Origin of the Samaritan Sect*. Cambridge, MA: Harvard University Press, 1968.

Pyles, Franklin Arthur. "The Missionary Eschatology of A. B. Simpson." In *The Birth of a Vision: Essays on the Ministry and Thought of Albert B. Simpson, Founder of The Christian and Missionary Alliance*, edited by David F. Hartzfeld and Charles Nienkirchen, 29–48. Beaverlodge, Alberta: Buena Book Services, 1986.

Robinson, James M., ed. *The Nag Hammadi Library in English: Translated and Introduced by Members of the Coptic Gnostic Library Project*. 4th rev. ed. Leiden: Brill, 1996.

Rashi. *Commentary on Avodah Zarah*. Sefaria. https://www.sefaria.org/Rashi_on_Avodah_Zarah.10a

Saint Murad. *Qur'an* (Saint Murad Translation). English digital edition. https://www.patreon.com/SaintMurad/shop/complete-package-quran-saint-murad-315350

Sara, Jack. "Replacement Theology Is a Heresy." *Come and See* (Opinion), November 13, 2025.

Schäfer, Peter. *Jesus in the Talmud*. Princeton, NJ: Princeton University Press, 2007.

Sanders, E. P. *Paul and Palestinian Judaism: A Comparison of Patterns of Religion*. Philadelphia: Fortress, 1977.

Schmidt, Karl Ludwig. "ἐκκλησία." In *Theological Dictionary of the New Testament*, edited by Gerhard Kittel and Gerhard Friedrich, translated by Geoffrey W. Bromiley, vol. 3, 501–536. Grand Rapids, MI: Eerdmans, 1965.

Segal, Alan F. *Two Powers in Heaven: Early Rabbinic Reports About Christianity and Gnosticism*. Leiden: Brill, 1977.

Schweitzer, Albert. *The Quest of the Historical Jesus*. Translated by W. Montgomery. New York: Macmillan, 1968. Originally published 1906.

Simpson, A. B. "Aggressive Christianity." *The Christian and Missionary Alliance Weekly* 23 (September 23, 1899): 260–62.

———.*Christ in the Bible*. New York: Word, Work and World, 1888.

———. *Days of Heaven Upon Earth: A Year Book of Scripture Texts and Living Truths*. New York: Christian Alliance, 1897.

Skarsaune, Oskar. *In the Shadow of the Temple: Jewish Influences on Early Christianity*. Downers Grove, IL: InterVarsity, 2002.

Soulen, R. Kendall. *The God of Israel and Christian Theology*. Minneapolis: Fortress, 1996.

Sproul, R. C. *John*. St. Andrew's Expositional Commentary. Kindle. Lake Mary, FL: Reformation Trust, 2016.

———. *The Last Days According to Jesus: Revised and Updated Edition: When Did Jesus Say He Would Return?* Grand Rapids, MI: Baker, 2008.

Stanley, Christopher D. *Paul and the Language of Scripture: Citation Technique in the Pauline Epistles and Contemporary Literature*. Cambridge: Cambridge University Press, 1992.

Staples, Jason A. *The Idea of Israel in Second Temple Judaism: A New Theory of People, Exile, and Israelite Identity*. Cambridge: Cambridge University Press, 2021.

Steinsaltz, Adin. *The Talmud: The Steinsaltz Edition*. New York: Random House, 1989–1999.

Stuckenbruck, Loren T. *The Myth of Rebellious Angels: Studies in Second Temple Judaism and New Testament Texts*. Tübingen: Mohr Siebeck, 2014.

Sutton, Matthew Avery. *American Apocalypse: A History of Modern Evangelicalism*. Cambridge, MA: Belknap, 2014.

Tabor, James D. *The Jesus Dynasty: The Hidden History of Jesus, His Royal Family, and the Birth of Christianity*. New York: Simon & Schuster, 2006.

———. *The Lost Mary: Rediscovering the Mother of Jesus*. New York: Knopf, 2025.

———. *Restoring Abrahamic Faith*. 4th ed., rev. and expanded. N.p.: Genesis 2000, 2025.

Van De Walle, Bernie A. *The Heart of the Gospel: A. B. Simpson, the Fourfold Gospel, and Late Nineteenth-Century Evangelical Theology*. Eugene, OR: Pickwick, 2009.

Wagenseil, Johann Christoph. *Tela Ignea Satanae: Hoc est, Arcani & Horribiles Judaeorum Adversus Christum Deum, & Christianam Religionem Libri Aneklotoi.* 5 pts. in 2 vols. Altdorf (Altdorfi Noricorum): J. H. Schönnerstaedt, 1681.

Warfield, Benjamin B. *Perfectionism.* 2 vols. New York: Oxford University Press, 1931.

Weber, Timothy P. *On the Road to Armageddon: How Evangelicals Became Israel's Best Friend.* Grand Rapids, MI: Baker Academic, 2004.

Whitehead, Andrew L., and Samuel L. Perry. *Taking America Back for God: Christian Nationalism in the United States.* New York: Oxford University Press, 2020.

WikiNoah English. "Main Page." https://www.wikinoah.org/en/index.php/Main_Page.

World Evangelical Alliance. "Arab Christian from Nazareth to Lead World Evangelical Alliance in Historic Appointment." October 30, 2025.

Wright, N. T. *Paul and the Faithfulness of God.* Christian Origins and the Question of God 4. Minneapolis: Fortress, 2013.

Wright, N. T., and Mark Kinzer. "Debate on the Meaning of Israel." MJTI School of Jewish Studies. https://www.youtube.com/watch?v=xDxENGsKaUQ

www.ingramcontent.com/pod-product-compliance
Lightning Source LLC
LaVergne TN
LVHW050641100826
845148LV00011B/1934
9798385274291

"This book is an excellent addition to the corpus of works dealing with preaching, especially expository preaching. Take up and read!"

—David L. Allen, Distinguished Professor of Practical Theology, Mid-America Baptist Theological Seminary

"*The Summons of the Text* offers a robust framework for text-driven preaching that grounds homiletical practice in deep theological conviction and biblical fidelity."

—Carl J. Bradford, Dean of Texas Baptist College

"With the mind of a scholar and the heart of a preacher, Dr. Gale addresses not only the need but also the requirement for every biblical sermon to include a call for response, offering practical and specific examples along the way."

—Adam L. Hughes, Associate Professor of Expository Preaching and Pastoral Leadership, New Orleans Baptist Theological Seminary

"Bruce Gale has given a much-needed gift to the church . . . This is not only a book I will recommend, but a book I will use in the training of pastors and preachers."

—J. Josh Smith, Pastor, Prince Avenue Baptist Church, Georgia

"In *The Summons of the Text*, Dr. Gale provides text-driven preachers with both the reasoning behind and rationale for summoning their hearers to respond to the meaning of every text they preach."

—Matt Queen, Associate Pastor, Plymouth Park Baptist Church, Texas

"[Gale] provides a historical, theological, and practical understanding of the summons and how it properly calls the listener, both believer and unbeliever, to respond to the biblical text."

—Kevin Ulmer, Evangelism Strategist, Louisiana Baptist Convention

"Dr. Bruce Gale reminds us that Scripture is not merely a source for sermons—it is the source that shapes and drives them. This work calls us back to preaching that is anchored in the text and responsive to its voice."

—Joshua Hughes, Senior Pastor, Beaver Dam Baptist Church, North Carolina

"Bruce Gale hits the mark by expanding the three pillars of text-driven preaching to include a fourth. This book challenges preachers and scholars alike to evaluate the biblical mandate of Scripture while integrating it into their preaching."

—Michael E. Newton, Business and Ministry Consultant

"Dr. Gale brilliantly addresses the heart of why we preach through this book. He calls readers to understand what a passage communicates and the passion the text summons so that they can better convey application. I highly recommend Gale's work for pastors and theologians alike."

—Dave McPherson, Senior Pastor, Southside Baptist Church, Oklahoma

"Bruce Gale's *The Summons of the Text* is a faithful and invaluable resource for anyone—especially pastors—who desires to rightly handle God's word. It is a strong and convicting reminder that Scripture does not merely inform, but also speaks with divine authority, reveals Christ Jesus, and calls hearers to respond with repentance, faith, obedience, and worship."

—Schylar B. Fields, Lead Pastor, Rosemont Baptist Church, Kentucky

"Through useful illustrations and examples from the word of God, [Gale] challenges us to look afresh at our preparation, presentation, and proclamation of the summons to faith in Christ."

—Bill Connors, Pastor, Eastern Hills Baptist Church, New Mexico